D1015606

THE HALF-LIFE OF AN AMERICAN ESSAYIST

The
Half-Life
of an
American
Essayist

by

ARTHUR KRYSTAL

DAVID R. GODINE · *Publisher*

BOSTON

First published in 2007 by
DAVID R. GODINE · *Publisher*
Post Office Box 450
Jaffrey, New Hampshire 03452
www.godine.com

LIBRARY OF CONGRESS CATALOGING-IN-PUBLICATION DATA
Krystal, Arthur.
The half-life of an American essayist : essays /
by Arthur Krystal. — 1st ed.
p.   cm.
ISBN-13: 978-1-56792-328-5
ISBN-10: 1-56792-328-3
I. Title.
PS3611.R96H36 2007
814'.54—dc22
2006102429

FIRST EDITION
Printed in the United States of America

Contents

What abortions are these Essays! What errors, what ill-pieced transitions, what crooked reasons, what lame conclusions! How little is made out, and that little how ill! Yet they are the best I can do.

— WILLIAM HAZLITT

Experience is only half of experience.

— JOHANN WOLFGANG VON GOETHE

The Half-Life
of an
American Essayist

SOMEHOW, without ever intending to, I've ended up a freelance intellectual. Not quite a man of letters, not really a critic anymore, but a sort of literary mule – a cross between haphazard journalist and restive seminarian. And it's no fun. Magazines that actually pay for the sort of things I write can be counted on the fingers of a hand that's encountered a sharp piece of machinery. I write, as it happens, essays with a literary bent, and though there are plenty of small periodicals that welcome such pieces, they pay honorariums of three hundred dollars or less. And since I'm unwilling to write, and probably incapable of writing, about more trendy subjects, I can forget about all the glossy magazines that pay quite well by a writer's standards.

Even a "successful" essayist, one who regularly places his or her work in the *New Yorker* and the *Atlantic*, will have a tough time getting a book of essays published. An essay may create a stir in a magazine, as Tom Wolfe's "Stalking The Billion-Footed Beast" did in 1988 when it appeared in *Harper's*, but essays in book form tend to cancel each other

I

out. No one buys a book because it contains a famous essay. This, of course, does not dissuade essayists from wanting to see their pieces collected; it just makes publishers leery of collecting them. Only if you're an established literary figure with a sizable fan base, whom publishers want to keep happy, will your scattered pieces rise and converge. No one, let me assure you, wants to keep me happy. Collected literary essays, especially, do not sell. They are hard to market, they receive very few reviews, and little, if anything, is spent on promoting them.

That said, I decided some years ago to publish a book of essays. My agent at the time wished me luck and washed his hands. So I did what all writers do when they start out: I made phone calls and I wrote letters. Editors at a number of publishing houses asked to see the work, but lost interest once they received it. "Hey, these really *are* literary essays. What was I thinking?" is what I imagine they said to themselves. In the end, Jonathan Brent, the editorial director of Yale University Press, decided to take a chance, and *Agitations: Essays on Life and Literature* found its way into the bookstores.

Bear in mind, these are, once again, literary pieces. None of this "creative non-fiction" nonsense, which is just a pretentious term for memoiristic writing. Although, commercially speaking, essay writing is a sucker's game, memoirs remain a draw; and if you've had the good fortune – from a writer's point of view – to have been abused as a child, survived a shipwreck or cancer, spent time in jail, or been addicted to internet porn, your chances of getting published are better than average. Memoirists simply write personal essays – period. Their work is no more creative than any other kind of essay; quite the reverse in fact. Writing interestingly about Jane Austen requires more imagination than confessing to having slept with someone named Jane Austen from Beaumont, Texas. And if I may say so, literary essayists have to rely more on their strengths as writers than on their imperfections as human beings – though I like to think I'm just as flawed and miserable as the next person.

Goethe, in an unusually pithy phrase, once summed up the literary life in this way: "Experience is only half of experience." I assume he meant by this that no experience is complete until it has been put through the intellectual wringer, which extracts every nuance and shade of meaning from what happens. As a writer, I believe that, temperamentally, I am better suited to the first half of experience. That is, I am disinclined to obsess over experience or write revealing essays about it. The end result is essays that book publishers don't want to touch – the essays in this volume, for example.

These particular pieces cover a lot of ground, ranging from laziness and physiognomy to the cultural implications of the typewriter, from boxing's appeal to writers to the growth of the Holocaust industry. Just try to get such pieces published in book form. Undaunted, I handed them over to my agent who, after glancing at them, was properly aghast. Publishers, he said, would think him "daft" for showing them such a book. He also informed me that I needed to get serious about what I wanted to achieve as a writer. Evidently, I needed "to write a real book," not just something that would flatter my vanity. All books, it strikes me, are vanity, but he was right about this particular book's prospects. Trade publishers turned it down right and left; always with misgivings, always with words of praise, always with best wishes. Only David R. Godine, an independent publisher who apparently likes bucking the tide, embraced the book's contents. Something about the voice of the essays made them seem more of a cohesive work than a collection of disparate pieces.

How does one end up being a professional writer without a book, without a sustained narrative of fiction or nonfiction? It's not that hard. All you need is a strong stomach for cheap food and a good education without a specific area of expertise. And let's not discount temperament, which is what people mean when they say you make your own luck. As luck would have it, I am not a writer of books, but of essays. Why essays? Well, for one thing, the essay seems to suit me. Unlike books, an essay has a perfect length, depending on the nature of its subject, and there is something eminently satisfying in finding that length. Moreover, an essay obviously takes less time to write than a book and it can do the job almost as well. Raymond Chandler once claimed that he would stick to essays if they paid enough.

And because the essay form is how I convey thoughts and impressions, I write pieces that journals and magazines sometimes publish, but that book publishers shy away from. Welcome to the wonderful world of the freelance writer. Although most writers know early on that the writing life is for them, none, I imagine, ever said to himself, "Please, God, let me be a freelancer." Freelancing is something you back into, usually because temperament and circumstance helpfully shove you along. One might even say that the very reasons one becomes a freelance writer are the reasons that make being a freelance writer so difficult: the desire to be independent, a hatred of authority, an aversion to regimen and, of course, the inability to play well with others. None of this matters when it comes to the actual writing, but it all, unfortunately, comes home to roost when dealing with editors, agents, and publishers.

Nobody really writes about the miseries, indignities, and small humiliations of being a marginal, albeit published, writer. Yes, writers are always bitching about how tough

4

things are, but they rarely voice their complaints in print. Maybe they're worried that magazine and book editors won't like what they read. Or maybe writers feel it's pointless to put into words what words cannot change. Well, I have no problem about grumbling out loud; I like to grumble and I'm too old to care if publishers take offense – which is highly doubtful.

There are more than a few things wrong with being a freelance writer, but let's begin with the obvious: *money* – there's not enough of it. While not all freelancers are hopelessly in debt – writers who cover fashion, fads, pop culture, sports, celebrities, and politics make out all right – those predisposed to write about books or ideas had better have a teaching gig or full-time job. Then there's *respect* – also not enough of it. Magazine and book editors don't go out of their way to make life miserable, but neither do they go out of their way to make it pleasant. Calls are not returned; letters remain unanswered; work lies unread. Finally: *lag time* – too much of it. To wait three months before hearing about a submission is not only annoying, it's draining fiscally and emotionally. If the article is timely and deals with a recent event or recently published book, you lose the chance to sell it elsewhere. An editor not liking my work doesn't bother me; an editor waiting three months to tell me he can't use the piece does. Do I feel rejected? No. What I feel is inconvenienced.

Writers who scrabble for a living come in three denominations: the midlist writer who generally writes better than the big-name writer but has a much smaller following; the even less well-known experimental writer who refuses to sell out and publishes in out-of-the-way journals with names like *Egg* or *Behemoth*; and the somewhat successful writer who publishes in all the "right" places, but never really breaks out. To fall into any of these categories is to encounter neglect, rudeness, and indifference.

It's toughest, of course, when you're just starting out. Writers take jobs as copy editors, fact checkers, waiters, and receptionists. When they're not marking up manuscripts or answering phones, they're scratching, hustling, and networking. It's not enough to have one's work out there, the body must be out there as well. And though you're hearing this from someone who never attended a writing school, writers' conference, or artists' colony – from someone who, as it happens, has burned bridges with a wet match – I know whereof I speak. My advice is: Be nice. Be nice to people with more power than you have, which means just about everyone. Get into the loop as soon as you can and befriend as many other writers as possible, since one of them may make it big one day. Never refuse an invitation to a book party and always show up wearing an Hermès tie and Carol Channing smile. And if you review books, be gentle as well as judicious. I know of at least two established writers who, when young, not only wrote well of other writers' books, they also wrote fawning letters to writers already famous. Slippery, but smart. But ... slippery.

Not that any of this will protect you from a simple truth about publishing: you may win an agent's or editor's respect, but common courtesy is extended only to those who fill the coffers. And for those who prefer courtesy to respect, this can be a problem. So what do you do? Well, the smart thing is to roll with the punches. A wrong step, a wrong word, and you will be cashiered out of the literary life for conduct unbecoming an unaffiliated writer. Of course, if you're a prickly individual who feels like punching back, you're in trouble. I may not get into a fistfight with a midget, as John O'Hara once did, but I'm quick to take offense and more than happy to return it. Anyway, you've got to admire a man who's not too big to fight a midget.

It also pays to know what editors want and give it to

them. Madonna has taken up the Kabbalah? Astonishing! Five thousand words would barely cover it. An ex-ballerina has written a book about the pleasures of sodomy? By God, it's time to burn the midnight oil. But what if you can't muster the enthusiasm? I, for one, don't see why more editors aren't interested in essays on death, despair, solitude, or Herman Broch's excellent study of Hugo von Hofmannsthal – but that's just me. That's another problem with being a freelance: you're never sure whether you're writing what you want to write or writing simply to pay the rent. For example, I wrote about the evolution and significance of the typewriter, but what if every editor I approached had thought it a dumb idea – would I have tackled the subject? Probably not. Then there were essays I wrote because of some fatuous statements made by Joyce Carol Oates about boxing and Raymond Chandler. Had I been rich, I might simply have written Ms. Oates a snide note or just ranted to friends. Don't get me wrong, I'm glad to have written these pieces, but I wrote them because there'd be a payday at the end.

There *are*, it should be said, some good points about being a freelance writer: You can sleep late, set your own hours, work at your own pace, and not worry about someone looking over your shoulder. On the other hand, you tend to sleep late, you have to set your own hours, you work only when you feel like it, and there is no one looking over your shoulder. Lest you think I'm cranky, let me say that I don't mind writing; I just mind writing for money. Yes, I'm aware that Dr. Johnson thought that "no man but a blockhead ever wrote, except for money." But I take a different view. Writing for money is work even when you're writing what it is you want to write. And if you're writing *only* for money, even a lot money, it's a tough way to make a living.

And maybe because writing seems to me both so important and so transparent (in the sense that it's demonstrably good or bad), I wonder how writers can go public with their work before it's ready. It's not journalists with deadlines I'm thinking of; they're like professional musicians who perform night after night – you expect a mistake now and then. Novelists, biographers, and historians, however, should be held to the same standards that apply to musicians during a studio recording. The tempo or interpretation may not be to your liking, but there's no excuse for dropped notes or extraneous noise.

The essayist has an advantage here: it's far easier to write a good essay than a good book. Most books – not just the ones identified by Henry James – *are* loose, baggy monsters. I can't go after monsters; I have neither the desire, nor the equipment, nor the *sitzfleish* required to do the work. But that doesn't mean I'm trying to get away with something. Quite the opposite. Because I don't like to work, I insist that whatever work I do be perfect. I'm not saying it is, but if I'm going to work at writing, then I ought to be happy with what I write. All of which makes me irascible – not because editors meddle with my work, but because I'm never quite satisfied with it.

Furthermore, because I am dour by nature, I can't help wondering if what I do is actually worth doing. I am, as I've written elsewhere, a veritable lazybones. And it occurs to me, as I write this, that laziness is a symptom of some deep-rooted pessimism, a feeling that, ultimately, actions don't matter – at least one's own actions don't. Optimists, of course, go forth into the world and tweak or chip away until the world, bit by bit, changes. Indeed, the world is buoyed by the enthusiasm and energy of such people. I seem to be talking about "such people" as if they comprised a different species. In a sense, they do. The lazy and the energetic, or the pessimistic and the optimistic, do not carry the same electrical charge. One acts, and the other watches (if it's not too much trouble).

In the days before psychiatry took the onus off melancholy (and the lazy *are* melancholic), virtue was equated with the work ethic. In such a world, the lazy were actually considered subversive. G. K. Chesterton went so far as to recommend the slammer for the hopelessly unhappy. In *The Man Who Was Thursday*, he imagines a "philosophical policeman" whose job "is at once bolder and more subtle than that of the ordinary detective. The ordinary detective goes to pot-houses to arrest thieves; [philosophical policemen] go to artistic tea-parties to detect pessimists."

I may be exaggerating my own laziness, but I can tell you from long experience that being an aimless, melancholic, bumptious freelance writer is not conducive to producing a large body of work. I may jump over many hurdles in publishing (or, more accurately, knock them over), but one thing I cannot always do is find things to write about. In thirty-odd essays, I've written about everything that has ever interested me. So why continue? Certainly if I had more money, I would write less. Maybe I'd write an essay with the title "Show Me Your Precursors," and – who knows? – maybe I *will* write a piece on Hermann Broch and Hugo von Hofmannsthal. On the other hand, there's a chance I'll just hang it up, or perhaps turn that hand to writing haiku; seventeen syllables and you're out.

That said, I believe in the essay, particularly the literary essay. I believe that in the right hands – those extending from the sleeves of Montaigne, Francis Bacon, Sir Thomas Browne, Samuel Johnson, Hazlitt, Orwell, Cyril Connolly, Virginia Woolf, Lionel Trilling and a dozen or so others – the literary essay, although it may begin by addressing books, always ends up being about the interaction of society and culture. And because language and thought are inseparable, I believe that the essay remains the artistic form in which consciousness achieves its fullest expression. All in all, not a bad way of making a bad living.

Typewriter
Days

I
N 1882, for the sum of 375 marks (plus shipping), Friedrich Wilhelm Nietzsche bought himself a typewriter. He didn't call it a typewriter; he called it a *schreibkugel* – literally, a "writing ball." The *schreibkugel* had been developed ("invented" is a tricky word when it comes to typewriters) sixteen years earlier by a Danish pastor and teacher of the deaf and dumb, Hans Rasmus Johann Malling Hansen. Impressed by the speed with which his students signed, Hansen figured they could also write faster if *all* their fingers were engaged; and inside of two years he produced a strangely elegant, convex-shaped writing machine that worked from top to bottom. The keys bore only capital letters and were arranged on rods in a semicircle at the top; when tapped, they thrust obliquely downward toward a common point on the platen, partially obscuring the paper that lay curved on a wheel rising from the machine's base. In effect, the typist could not see what was being typed. Nietzsche, whose own eyesight was famously weak and getting worse, was thrilled with his new possession: "THE

WRITING BALL IS A THING LIKE ME: MADE OF / IRON / YET EASILY TWISTED ON JOURNEYS," he pecked out. Unfortunately, for the novice *Maschinen-schreiber*, the writing ball soon went kaput, and Nietzsche, uncomplainingly, went back to his pens. Still, six weeks of use was all he needed to form the conclusion (dutifully typed): "Our writing tools are also working on our thoughts."

If Nietzsche was the first philosopher to use the typewriter, Friedrich Kittler, a professor of aesthetics and media studies at Berlin's Humboldt University, is the first philosopher of the typewriter. Well, perhaps not *the* first. Heidegger's *Parmenides* contains some portentous fritterings about the typewriter's ascendancy over the hand, but these consist of just a few pages, and they were composed by hand. Kittler is a keyboard man; he has to be, given the short time between his *Discourse Networks 1800/1900* (1985) and *Gramophone, Film, Typewriter* (1986), both of which describe, at some length, the transmutation of values following the changeover from handwriting to typewriting around the turn of the twentieth century. Fascinating as that sounds, I'm afraid I cannot recommend Kittler's books unless you are over twenty-one or enrolled in a Critical Theories program where theory reigns over art.

Of course, if you are under twenty-one you have probably never used a typewriter except to fill out an application, and consequently the loud *thwack* of typewriter keys striking a cylindrical roller and the satisfying *ping* of the carriage reaching the end of the track are not in your mnemonic repertoire. In fact, all that you are likely to have in common with those who grew up using the typewriter is a woeful ignorance of its historical ramifications, which are considerable and consistent with an object that at one time was the most complex mass-produced machine in America.

The reason it is hard to say who invented the typewriter

is that the idea of a writing machine seems to have been in the waters during the first half of the nineteenth century. Patents were being issued all over the place for dinguses and doohickeys that promised to deliver letters of the alphabet to a piece of paper with only minimal assistance from an operator. They arrived bearing such piquant names as *Machine Kryptographique*, *Tachigraph*, *Mechanical Potenographo*, *Cembalo Scrivano* (Writing Harpsichord), *Typographer*, and *Chirographer*; and they resembled sewing machines, guillotines, mousetraps, spinning tops, miniature printing presses, and small pianos (*pianos à écrire*). By the third quarter of the century, the basic elements of the typewriter were in place. Along with Hansen's writing ball, there were John Pratt's 1864 Pterotype, important enough to be written up in *Scientific American*, and a series of technically sound machines built by Peter Mitterhofer, an Austrian carpenter, whose Merano Model of 1867 looks like something out of Fritz Lang's *Metropolis*.

The "fifty-second man" to invent the typewriter, according to Bruce Bliven Jr.'s *The Wonderful Writing Machine*, was an old newspaperman and printer named Christopher Latham Sholes. Huddled with his partners, Carlos Glidden and Samuel W. Soule, in a Milwaukee machine shop during the summer of 1867, Sholes pieced together what would become the first commercial typewriter in America. Six years later, after various kinks had been worked out, the Type-Writer was ready for production. The 1873 apparatus had a four-bank keyboard, type bars that hung in a circle beneath the cylindrical platen, and a lead ball suspended from one side, whose weight moved the carriage. (The ball would later be dropped in favor of a treadle table and foot pedal.) Applying an "up-strike" type-bar motion, similar to a pianoforte's hammers jutting toward the strings, the Milwaukee typewriter was a "blind machine," the paper descending into the works as the type bar rose to meet it. The only way to see the print was by raising the hinged carriage or waiting until you had typed three or four lines.

It was a serviceable device, but apparently not a commercial one. In desperation, Sholes offered Thomas Edison a partnership, but Edison, busy with his own inventions, politely declined. Sholes then turned to a pair of savvy businessmen, who proceeded first to buy him out, and second to persuade the New York firearm firm of E. Remington & Sons to redesign the machine and market it. As it happened, the gun industry was ideally suited to this purpose. Already distinguished by specialized tools, precise gauges, and the interchangeability of parts, Remington & Sons quickly went from producing standardized weapons parts to making writing instruments. It's not for nothing – and not just because of the rattling of small hammers striking a platen – that Kittler calls the typewriter "a discursive machine gun." In 1874, the first Remington-built Sholes & Glidden Type Writer (somewhere along the line Soule seems to have been misplaced) was shipped.

Despite its best efforts, Remington managed to sell only 550 machines the first year and another 4,500 between 1875 and 1878. One problem may have been the Remington slogan, "to save time is to lengthen life"; another was that the annual per capita income in the United States at the time was around $125, or roughly the cost of a new typewriter. The newfangled machines were interesting, but were they practical? Although it seems perfectly obvious now, not many people in 1867, including the typewriter's inventors, envisioned its full potential. According to the evolutionary biologist Jared Diamond, inventions sometimes have less to do with necessity than with tinkerers designing

and building contraptions because – well, because that's
what tinkerers do. And only after they've come up with a
new technology do they or someone else find a sensible
application for it. So Remington's sales continued to be
sluggish – until, suddenly, they weren't; and the reason
was as plain as the red polish on manicured fingernails.

In 1881 the New York City chapter of the YWCA
trained eight young women to become typists. Upon grad-
uation, they were promptly snapped up at $10 per week.
Until that time, a woman with an education might become
a teacher, governess, or nurse; the rest had to be satisfied
with jobs as seamstresses, servants, shopgirls, or mill hands,
earning anywhere from $1.50 to $8 for a week's labor.
Office work was a long shot at best; in 1870 fewer than
4 percent of all clerical workers were women. No lady
scriveners kept Bartleby company. It was the typewriter
that pushed open the brass-plated doors of law, commerce,
and government offices and invited – nay, solicited – the
female sex. Soon middle-class girls were slipping into their
starched white shirtwaists, marching into a place of business, sitting down at their "office pianos," and eventually
standing up as private secretaries, bank tellers, account-
ants, and managers. So many, in fact, availed themselves of
this new opportunity that by 1900 nearly 75 percent of all
clerical workers in America were women (Bliven puts the
number, in 1888, at sixty thousand); and for decades the
typist and her machine were both called "typewriters."

The armada of women who sailed into the workplace just
before the turn of the century did not go unnoticed. For
one thing, typewriters began flying out of the factories. In
1900 alone, around one hundred thousand Remingtons were
shipped, and by 1906 the Remington plant was turning out
a machine every working minute. With businesses everywhere demanding new and improved machines, tinkerers

like Sholes and Glidden stepped back, and entrepreneurs and mechanical engineers stepped forward. Soon Remington & Sons found itself competing with thirty other typewriter manufacturers, notably the John T. Underwood Company, which introduced, in 1895, a "front-strike" or "visible" machine that displayed the letters as soon the ribbon touched the paper. Six years later, Underwood cornered the market with its famous No. 5 model, which offered both a ribbon selector and a back spacer.

As for the office itself, men and women now found themselves on uncharted terrain, often behind closed doors, which, as it turned out, was a great boon to cartoonists ("Don't hold supper, dear. I'll be working late with my typewriter"), though not much of one to the cuspidor industry, which dried up under the baleful glare of the less expectorating sex. Needless to say, so many women working alongside men — becoming, in fact, indispensable to their male employers — had civic consequences. Once women began joining the workforce in such numbers, could universal suffrage and an Equal Rights Amendment be far behind?

And you never gave the typewriter a serious thought, did you? Maybe in your formative years you wondered why the sky is blue, or, more recently, who's buying those millions of Britney Spears CDs, but did you stop even once to consider the keyboard? The letters, be assured, didn't just fall out of the blue sky and jump up to arrange themselves along three rows. In the beginning was the alphabet, and it appeared on the first keyboards from left to right and from top to bottom — a sensible arrangement, since anyone wanting to use the machine would already know her ABCs and have no trouble locating them. But there was a problem: adjoining keys on the early machines tended to jam. Instead of adjusting the mechanism, Sholes and his partners simply scattered the most frequently used letters all over the keyboard, while concentrating some of them on the left side where the nondominant hand works. This configuration – the one that just about everyone in the Western world now uses – is known as QWERTY (after the first six letters on the uppermost alphabet row) and is, writes Bliven, both "madly inconvenient" and "considerably less efficient than if the arrangement had been left to simple chance."

QWERTY, adopted initially by some, but not all, manufacturers, was given a leg up in 1888 when the Shorthand and Typewriter Institute of Cincinnati sponsored a contest between Remington's QWERTY keyboard and a layout used by the American Writing Machine Company's Caligraph model. If typewriter historians are to be believed, the media were alerted. "The duel was widely reported all over the world," Wilfred A. Beeching writes in his *Century of the Typewriter*. Representing Remington was Frank E. McGurrin; in the Caligraph corner, using a double keyboard, the gallant Louis Traub. But, alas, like so many typewriting showdowns, this one did not live up to its billing. Not only could McGurrin touch-type blindfolded using all ten fingers, poor Traub was proficient only with eight. For an unscientific way of determining a keyboard's efficiency, this one is hard to beat. Nevertheless, when the Toronto Typewriters' Congress of 1888 advocated the standardization of the keyboard, nearly all manufacturers switched over to QWERTY.

Sholes's design, once entrenched, proved impossible to dislodge. In 1932, August Dvorak, a professor of education at the University of Washington in Seattle, slung the letters of the alphabet together in a new variant based on "scientific" principles. Meaning to bury that other "primitive tortureboard," Dvorak claimed that his design could increase typing speed by 35 percent and significantly reduce errors. Situating the five vowels and the five most commonly used consonants – A O E U I D H T N S – on the home or middle row, Dvorak predicted that about four hundred of the most common words could be typed without ever leaving "home," as compared with only around one hundred using the QWERTY keyboard. Instead of the fingers traveling between twelve and twenty miles over the QWERTY terrain during an average day's work, they could perform the same tasks in about a mile.

18

Official vindication arrived during World War II in the form of tests run by the U.S. Navy, with results favoring Dvorak's layout over Sholes's. In 1953, however, the United States General Services Administration conducted its own tests and found that a good typist was equally at home on both home rows. Dvorak's supporters were unfazed and maintain to this day that QWERTY is nothing less than "a feat of anti-engineering" that owes its longevity to the fact that it has become a fixture of the marketplace. Challenging QWERTY, Dvorak groused, was like asking people to "reverse the Ten Commandments and the Golden Rule, discard every moral principle, and ridicule motherhood!"

QWERTY may, in fact, be like a weaker mutant of a species that survives mainly because all the other animals have gotten used to it. But it also turns out that some of the professor's tests were rigged and that even the U.S. Navy's data was flawed. In a 1990 paper, "The Fable of the Keys," Stan Leibowitz and Stephen Margolis dispute the imputation that QWERTY is a textbook example of economic "lock-in." Instead they contend that Dvorak's layout possesses no clear-cut advantage, or at least not enough of one to warrant the economic effort that a wholesale switchover would require.

Whatever its demerits, QWERTY has already outlived the machine for which it was designed. The typewriter is nearly obsolete, and pretty soon even die-hard users will be gone. What will remain? A bunch of antiques in museums and private collections, and perhaps the typewriter lore that has grown up around them. Mark Twain, it seems, mistakenly identified *Tom Sawyer* as the first typewritten book manuscript (scholars believe it was his *Life on the Mississippi*). Soon thereafter, a clever Petrograd salesman obtained a photograph of a grumpy-looking Count Tolstoy dictating to his daughter, who sits poised in front of a Remington. In Arthur Conan Doyle's 1892 story, "A Case of Identity," a typewriter is used to solve the murder; and in Erik Satie's 1917 ballet *Parade*, one can hear the rapid clicking of typewriter keys. And, finally, who can forget the wild 1923 fight between Jack Dempsey and Luis Firpo, when Dempsey, after getting knocked through the ropes by Firpo (memorialized in George Bellows's famous lithograph), climbed back into the ring by stepping on a portable Corona? In a Timex-typewriter moment, the machine continued to perform, delighting its manufacturers, who promptly took out an ad: "Dempsey knocked out Firpo, but he could not knock out Corona!" No, time will not backspace typewriter buffs' affections. For them, Royal, Hammond, and Blickensderfer ("the Blick") will always possess the élan of such classic automobile monikers as Pierce Arrow, Stutz Bearcat, and Duesenberg.

It would be a stretch to call Friedrich Kittler an aficionado of the typewriter's rack-and-pinion escapement, but then Kittler doesn't pretend to be interested in the cuddly appeal of technology; his quarry is the wide-ranging and elusive destinies of communication systems that have become woven into the fabric of daily life. If you detect a strong whiff of Marshall McLuhan here, you're probably old enough to remember students and journalists running around in the mid-sixties, declaiming that the medium is the message, while pointing out which media are "hot" (radio) and which "cool" (TV). Yet in all that techno-aesthetic hubbub, no one seems to have noticed a little item tucked away in *Understanding Media*. I refer to McLuhan's sneaky implication that modernism is essentially a byproduct of the typewriter.

To hear McLuhan tell it, the typewriter contributed to T. S. Eliot's colloquial bends and dips in *Sweeney Agonistes*, to Ezra Pound's syncopated rhythms, and to E. E. Cummings's punctuationless, zigzagging verse. "Seated at the typewriter, the poet, much in the manner of the jazz musician, has the experience of performance as composition," McLuhan writes. Not only does the typewriter fuse "composition and publication, causing an entirely new attitude to the written and printed word"; it gives the illusion of impersonality and anonymity, thereby freeing the poet, and sometimes the novelist, to improvise, to say things that the hand might hesitate to commit to paper. Give a poet a typewriter, McLuhan says, and he will start doing "Nijinsky leaps or Chaplin-like shuffles and wiggles. . . . Composing on the typewriter is like flying a kite."

Another writer cited by McLuhan who came to rely on the typewriter, though one who kept his kite on a tight string, was Henry James. The Master, of course, did not himself type, but dictated to a Miss Theodora Bosanquet, who faithfully transcribed on a Remington the circumvolutions, qualifications, and "hanging fire[s]" that the elderly James was committing to posterity. In fact, James got so used to dictating that he reached a point where he couldn't compose without the clatter of typewriter keys. And when his Remington broke down, he had a hard time making the transition to an Oliver typewriter because of the different sound the two machines made.

Kittler also adduces James and Eliot as writers whose work was affected by the typewriter, but Kittler takes McLuhan up a notch, which is saying something, given that McLuhan once likened himself to "Louis Pasteur telling doctors that their greatest enemy was quite invisible, and quite unrecognized by them." For Kittler, the medium is not only the message, it's pretty much the only message. "Media determine our situation," Kittler states blandly at the beginning of *Gramophone, Film, Typewriter*. As part of a new "discourse network," the typewriter helped end handwriting's monopoly over verbal communication; and, like film and sound recording, it exemplified the idea that the more we rely on technology, the further removed we become from a discourse that allows us to say directly what we think and feel. In sum, technology inevitably modifies our definition of humanness. Once a machine, for instance, replaces a human limb in the performance of a task, the relationship between task and man changes, as does the relationship between man and his formerly task-specific limb. "The typewriter tears writing from the essential realm of the hand," Heidegger had cautioned. "The typewriter veils the essence of writing and of the script. It withdraws from man the essential rank of the hand."

Our first instinct may be to scoff at such pronouncements, but there is a kernel of truth here. Forty years ago, in what seems now like another age, penmanship denoted breeding, education, and character. The Palmer Method of teaching handwriting, an essential part of most schools' curricula, accustomed the hand to making graceful loops and swirls, the better to send it out into a world where an illegible scrawl was considered rude and a fine Italianate hand was a mark of distinction. Because handwriting was an extension of personality, correspondence was personal even when nothing of a personal nature was being communicated, and this awareness remains with us. Even now we tend not to type love letters or e-mail condolence notes; we sense that such communiqués require the hand's, not merely the writer's, signature.

22

But what of the poet's or the novelist's signature, that is to say, consciousness? Did it, too, undergo a transformation? Something happened, after all, when writers began to type. Instead of using a slender cylindrical object that fit snugly between their fingers, they began to compose on a boxy machine that presents discrete letters of the alphabet separated by spaces. Instead of words in ink flowing from the tip of a pen, printed letters appear by mechanical means in a place apart from where the hand works. Instead of the wrist lowering a quill into the dark recess of an inkwell, it remains hovering over a keyboard. Gone, too, is the sound of a quill moving across foolscap; gone, the role of the non-dominant hand that holds and adjusts the paper, thus framing the movement of the writing hand. Surely all this once counted for something.

What, though? The hand is obviously more than an appendage that sports a pinky ring or scratches a mosquito bite, and anyone who takes it for granted should get his mitts on Frank R. Wilson's *The Hand* and marvel at the complex cognitive, neurological, and anthropological transactions that go into a simple manual gesture. That said, it isn't the moving hand that writes, it's the entire physiology of the hand's owner; and this is where media theorists charge in. Writing by hand and typing are not the same, Kittler insists. Just look at what happened to Nietzsche's rhetoric after six weeks at his writing ball: his arguments turned into aphorisms, his thoughts into puns, his rhetoric into "a telegram style."

TYPEWRITER DAYS

The question needs asking: does a writer's style depend on the tools he uses? Style, after all, derives from "stylus" (from the Latin, *stilus*, meaning any sharp, pointed implement used for writing, drawing, or engraving). McLuhan wasn't entirely off base when he attributed certain stylistic refinements to the typewriter. "I am sloughing off all my long sentences which I used to dote upon," wrote the author of "The Waste Land," who ended up with "short, staccato [lines], like modern French prose." But if the typewriter affected the texture of poetry and prose, did it liquidate "the basis of classical authorship," as Kittler would have us believe? Did it somehow create "standardized texts" in which "paper and body, writing and soul fall apart"? (Is Hemingway, standing at his typewriter, less of a classical author than Ronald Firbank?) The divine afflatus may have given a small shudder when confronted with this quotidian apparatus, but it quickly composed itself.

Literature is not a slave to its tools: a writer with a pen and pad is not analogous to an artist with a sketchbook, or a musician with an instrument. Print, its type and font, is simply not the point of writing. It's absurd to think that Robert Browning, wielding a quill, felt himself more of a poet than Robert Graves, who, by the way, had a warm regard for his typewriter: "A veteran typewriter of which you have grown fond seems to reciprocate your feelings, and even encourage the flow of thought." Graves wrote, "At first, a lifeless assemblage of parts, it eventually comes alive." There are, as Orwell pointed out, some ideas that only an intellectual could believe in. As if to nail down his thesis that "Remington's and Underwood's invention ushered in a poetics that William Blake or John Donne with their limit/ears could not hear," Kittler quotes from D. J. Enright's tongue-in cheek *The Typewriter Revolution*:

The typeriter is crating
A revlootion in poetry
Pishing back the frontears
And apening up fresh feels
Unherd of by Done or Bleak

Yeah, that's what makes modernist poetry different: the typewriter.

Nietzsche's aperçu that our writing tools contribute to our thoughts sounds good; it's also partially true. Kittler's idea that our writing tools write us doesn't sound so good; what's more, it isn't true. There is a clear demarcation between the reasons we write and the tools we use to write, and the human need to express oneself in language surely overrides the means that satisfy this need. When Truman Capote slammed *On the Road* by referring to it as "type-writing," he chose the word not because the novel was composed on a continuous scroll of paper funneled through a typewriter, but because Capote assumed Kerouac hadn't paid much attention to the book's narrative style. He was blaming not the machine but its operator.

Ever since Walter Benjamin's famous essay of 1936, "The Work of Art in the Age of Mechanical Reproduction," a certain caste of intellectual has been throwing suspicious glances at the environment. Apparently, no object, however ordinary, is exempt when it comes to shaping our views and values. Benjamin, of course, did not intend to spawn an academic industry that looked at, around, or under our beds; he wished only to record that

during long periods of history, the mode of human sense perception changes with humanity's entire mode of existence. The manner in which human sense perception is organized, the medium in which it is accomplished, is determined not only by nature but by historical circumstances as well.

This seems a fair assessment. History has its way with us, and sense perception may periodically undergo transformations, as it did after Brunelleschi and Alberti rediscovered the art of linear perspective in the early fifteenth century. Nonetheless, we should not assume that every change in our habitat, whether it occurs naturally or arrives in the form of time-saving devices, or increasingly faster and more pervasive means of communication, radically changes human nature itself. Our children may be different from us for having grown up using the computer, but they're not *that* different.

Human beings evolve over the course of time, and successive generations may view, or at least represent, the world in different terms. Philosophers of the media, however, would have us evolve more quickly, as if, at this very instant, the electronic media were zapping us into becoming a mutant of our former selves. Evidently, the more we tinker with technology, the more technology tinkers with us. It's hard to argue with this, but whatever adjustments we make to a world that is too much with us, one aspect, perhaps the most important aspect, of being human does not change: namely, a mighty resistance to anything that makes us feel less human. That's why we don't like the idea of cloning ourselves, or of fashioning robots that bear us more than a passing resemblance. Individuality is part of what makes us human; and even if you've got nothing else, at least you've got a self that *is* no one else. And when you come down to it, Henry James dictating to a typist is still, and perhaps even more, Henry James.

The Pages
of Sin

THE BAD NEWS is that we are born sinners; the good news ("gospel" literally means good news) is that we can make things right through repentance. So Scripture, or the Catholic Church, tells us. It also tells us that along with sin there is Sin. Original sin, about which we can do nothing (except strive for grace), issues from man's first disobedience. Eve ate of the apple, enticed Adam to eat of it as well, and all of us, as a result, are rotten at the core. God, however, does not refer to this as a sin; rather it was Augustine of Hippo who peered closely and identified the hereditary stain on our souls. The word "sin" actually makes its first appearance in the Bible (Genesis 4:7) after Cain becomes angry with God for favoring Abel's offering of choice cuts of meat over Cain's own assortment of fruit. God doesn't care for Cain's attitude and says: "If you do not do well, sin is couching at the door; its desire is for you, but you must master it."

By then, however, it was too late. The apple had done its work: Cain invited Abel out to the field and, in time, as men multiplied over the face of the earth, wickedness and

violence were everywhere. Properly vexed, He sent His
flood, sparing only the six-hundred-year-old Noah, his wife
and sons, his sons' wives, and some animals. This should
have been enough to give Noah's descendants pause – but,
no, they too acted up, behaving sodomishly and gomorrishly,
praying to false gods and the like. This time, however, God
restrained Himself. Instead of wiping out the race of men,
He gave them His Ten Commandments, the first doctrinal
instance of supernal rules of behavior, from which our concept of the sins derives. In addition to instructions about
honoring God and parents and keeping the Sabbath, there
are those well-known but woefully ineffective proscriptions
against murder, adultery, stealing, lying, coveting, and lust-
ing. How, one can't help wondering, have we avoided
another flood?

Christianity offers one answer: God sent us Jesus instead.
It is Christ who came to suffer for our sins and to cleanse us
of them. Whether or not we avail ourselves of the opportunity, Jesus certainly altered how we regard sin. The sin that
wends its way through the Old Testament usually takes the
form of flouting God's will; it seems more a dereliction of
duty – rather brave and exceedingly stupid, considering
Yahweh's obvious bad temper – than an absence of faith.
It also appears as something external to man, something
"couching at the door." Jesus, however, saw sin differently
and put it where it belongs: in us. Whereas Yahweh demands
strict obedience, Jesus expects something besides: "You
have heard that it was said to the men of old, 'You shall not
kill; and whoever kills shall be liable to judgment.' But I
say to you that everyone who is angry with his brother
shall be liable to judgment." The Sermon on the Mount is
nothing less than a corrective to the Ten Commandments. If
the Commandments told man how to behave, the Sermon
told him how to feel.

Unfortunately, Christ's life and death did not automatically generate a radiant and immutable theology. As Christianity evolved over the course of several centuries, the Church fathers not only leaned on the teachings of the apostles, they also borrowed from Pharisaic texts, Hellenistic mystery cults, and Neoplatonic cosmology. Ecclesiastical councils were convened to determine whether Jesus' body was as divine as his spirit, and whether he was equal to, or only a subset of, God. Teachings that disagreed with the councils' findings were quickly declared heresies, and those who espoused contrary doctrines were excommunicated. The Church may have been built upon the rock that was Peter, but it found its hierarchic perspective in the caves of Plato and the writings of Aristotle. If God's rule is Judaic and God's love is Christian, then God's reason is Greek.

In a world created by an all-powerful intelligence, order and symmetry presided. Nature consisted of a series of graded existences from the simplest to the most complex, from the lowest and basest to the highest and best. The Church fathers, therefore, took a dim view of anything that distorted this picture or that obscured its beauty and wisdom – a perspective that continued well into the Enlightenment. Worshipping the world was simply another way of worshipping God, and as long as one didn't grasp at earthly pleasures at the expense of seeing the bigger picture, one could live securely on terra firma.

Sin was where man went wrong in a world that was ultimately right. Given what we know about the institutionalization of church doctrine, it's tempting to be irreverent about sin. But one would be wrong to scoff, at least where the early followers were concerned. For them, Jesus was the penultimate eschatological event – the one preceding Judgment Day, which clearly was not far off. Would God take the time to send His only begotten Son if time were not short? The first generations of Christians had every expectation of a new world that they or their children would live to see. Sin was thus doubly meaningful because not only was their own end nigh, the world's was, too, and they wanted to be prepared when both inevitabilities occurred.

Sin, therefore, had to do more than lead to punishment; it had to confirm the rightness of the world (by swerving away from it.) Having gotten its philosophical bearings, the Church decided that fear of hell, although necessary, was not sufficient. If Reason (could God be anything else?) moved the spheres and kept everything in alignment, if Reason extended even to the workings of hell, then the reason not to sin was Reason itself. Thoughts and behavior offensive to God were thus an affront to nature, a small tear in the divine fabric, and where nature was concerned one did not so much make distinctions as take inventory of those that already existed. There were four basic elements, ten heavenly spheres, four cardinal humors, four classical virtues, seven Christian virtues, and a specific number of sins. You could fiddle with the list, but there had to be a list.

With that established, the Church could turn its compartmentalizing mind to defining rules and responsibilities, assigning values to various kinds of behavior. So how many sins were there and what were their respective degrees of badness? Proverbs notes:

> There are six things which the LORD hates,
>   seven which are an abomination to him;
> haughty eyes, a lying tongue, and hands that
>   shed innocent blood,
> a heart that devises wicked plans, feet that make
>   haste to run to evil,

> a false witness who breathes out lies, and a man
> who sows discord among brothers.

Theft and adultery are absent, but there were still the Commandments, the Sermon on the Mount, and the apostles, who had plenty to say about sinning. Basically, there was no shortage of sins for the Church fathers to choose from, and if they required assistance, Paul né Saul was only too happy to oblige them. In his Epistle to the Colossians, Paul denounces "fornication, impurity, passion, evil desire, and covetousness, which is idolatry ... anger, wrath, malice, slander, and foul talk." In Romans, he comes down equally on same-sex relations, envy, murder, strife, deceit, malignity, gossip, slander, insolence, haughtiness, disobedience, foolishness, heartlessness, and ruthlessness. Fine distinctions were not Paul's forte; in Corinthians, he lumps the effeminate with liars, thieves, and extortionists. A pattern emerges: "If you live according to the flesh you will die, but if by the Spirit you put to death the deeds of the body, you will live" (Romans 8:13).

Over time, Scripture's cautionary words about behavior would become canonical law with only slight variations between Jews and Christians (mainly in the matter of conjugal relations). But before the sins became Seven or Deadly, they were first Cardinal or Capital and amounted to eight. In written form they materialize in the works of Evagrius Ponticus, a Greek monk (c. 345–399), who identified in men eight "evil thoughts." John Cassian (c. 360–434), another monk, soon Latinized these thoughts as eight *vitia* or faults; in ascending order of seriousness they were: *gula* (gluttony), *luxuria* (lust), *avarita* (avarice), *tristita* (sadness), *ira* (anger), *acedia* (spiritual lethargy), *vana gloria* (vanity), and *superbia* (pride). Cassian also proposed that each sin summons the next one in the chain.* ("Summon" because the sins were identified with external demonic forces that could enter and poison the mind.) Two centuries later, Pope Gregory I (c. 540–604) officially adopted the list, modifying it slightly by folding vainglory into pride, merging lethargy and sadness, and adding envy. Pride now became the sin responsible for all the others (an idea later taken up by Thomas Aquinas), and, from bad to worst, Gregory's list includes lust, gluttony, avarice, sadness (or melancholy), anger, envy, and pride. (Sloth would replace sadness only in the seventeenth century.)

Still, there remained the business of classification. Catholic dogma divides sin into two general categories – commission and omission – and, in each case, the malice and gravity must be determined. As regards malice, sins may partake of ignorance, passion, and infirmity; as regards gravity, sins are either mortal or venial (pardonable). "All wrongdoing is sin, but there is sin which is not mortal" (1 John 5:17). A mortal, or cardinal, sin was defined by Augustine as *Dictum vel factum vel concupitum contra legem aeternam* – something said, done, or desired contrary to the eternal law. Thus, a mortal sin is always voluntary, whereas a venial sin may contain little or no malice or be committed out of ignorance.†

---

* Although there is no exact counterpart to the seven sins in Jewish literature, a rabbinic midrash (an instance of scriptural exegesis) enumerates seven successive steps leading to an individual's downfall, beginning with the refusal to study Torah and concluding with the denial of God Himself.

† *The Catholic Encyclopedia* states: "No mortal sin is committed in a state of invincible ignorance or in a half-conscious state."

Conceived by monks for monks, the seven deadly sins took hold in the popular imagination, though probably not in equal measure. One can see how lust and gluttony would be a bother in a monastery, but should the secular poor not dig in if the opportunity presented itself? Still, the unmagnificent seven were a handy compendium, available to priests, parents, poets, and artists. Breughel, Bosch, Donizetti, Dante, Rabelais, Spenser, and John Bunyan took the seven as a subject, and neither by pen nor brush did they let them off lightly. Sin sent you straight to hell, where freezing water awaited the envious; dismemberment, the angry; snakes, the lazy; boiling oil, the greedy; fire and brimstone, the lustful. The sins, it bears repeating, were real external influences, and they were waiting for you.

Sinfulness may be absolute, but the respective gravity of individual sins was subject to historical conditions. Greed, for example, became a more serious transgression during the late Middle Ages when nobles enriched themselves at the expense of peasants without tithing to the church. And sloth came to be seen as worse than gluttony during the nineteenth century when more hands were needed to keep the wheels of industry spinning. For the most part, the seven deadlies were venial and therefore enjoyed some latitude. Mortal sin, though, was another matter. "The true nature of sin," according to *The Catholic Encyclopedia*, "is found perfectly only in a personal mortal sin, in other sin imperfectly."

Aquinas, who did his Aristotelian best to elucidate the finer points of sin, reserves "mortal" for offenses committed against nature (e.g., murder and sodomy); for exploiting the less fortunate; and for defrauding workmen of their wages, which nicely raises the stakes when screwing over one's employees. Mortal also splits into the spiritual (blasphemy) and the carnal (adultery), the commission of which puts a stain (macula) on the soul. The sins of the flesh, born of the flesh, however, are less serious than sins of the spirit. In fact, the greater the carnal nature of the sin, Aquinas reasons, the less culpability is involved. Oddly enough, Paul might agree, since he's pretty sure that nothing good dwells within the flesh and though he "can will what is right, [he] cannot do it." So if Paul does what he doesn't want to do, it's sin, not himself, that's at fault.

Sin, of course, became even less manageable during the Reformation. In fact, the very words Luther overheard that led to his break from the Church were "I believe in the forgiveness of sins." But what did that mean exactly? Only that forgiveness was not in our power to effect. In general terms, Protestant doctrine – which, of course, rejected the Church as the intermediary between God and man, thereby rejecting the Church's right to forgive our sins – held that the fulfillment of God's will cannot be affected by *our* will. Grace, in other words, comes about not through good works but through the goodness of God, about which we cannot presume. Sin exists: live with it, die with it, and hope that God forgives you for it. That doesn't mean you can do as you like, but it does mean that confession – however good for the soul – isn't good enough for absolution. One may surrender the self to God, in which case grace may miraculously descend, but it will *not* be as a reward for such surrender. Thus a certain helplessness exists not only in having been born in sin but also in being unable to do anything about it.

Tellingly, Jesus himself doesn't really harp on sin. Sin is regrettable, to be sure, but also pardonable. There is, however, one sin that is unforgivable: "Every sin and blasphemy will be forgiven men," Jesus says in Matthew 12:31–32, but ... "whoever speaks against the Holy Spirit will not be

forgiven, either in this age or in the age to come." The unforgivable sin makes the seven deadly ones look piddling by
comparison. And, truth to tell, the seven sins are not in and
of themselves all that exciting; it's what frenzied or slothful
people *do* with them that's peculiar or outrageous. Angry?
Envious? Lustful? Well, who hasn't been? Moreover, who
cares? Certainly an excess of any one of the sins, or some
nasty combination of them, may not win you friends, but
who truly believes that the bad-tempered, the envious, or
the lazy are going to hell? Even the all-too-pleasant idea of
bastards like Mengele or Stalin eternally roasting together
is credited only by scriptural literalists.

34

If the seven deadlies don't exactly make us quake in our
boots, they can at least serve as fodder for the literati. Ian
Fleming certainly thought so when, as a member of the editorial board of the London *Times* in the late 1950s, he asked,
among other luminaries, W. H. Auden, Cyril Connolly, and
Angus Wilson to weigh in on a particular sin. The result-
ing smallish book might be described, if one were given to
verbal raffishness, as sinfully entertaining. The essays are
urbane, knowing, and casual – one or two almost too casual
– and bear out Fleming's own assessment: "How drab and
empty life would be without these sins, and what dull dogs
we all would be without a healthy trace of many of them in
our make up!"

Of the seven contributors, only Auden (on anger) and
Evelyn Waugh (on sloth) take a marked exception to their
subjects, perfectly understandable given their religious
beliefs. Waugh takes the lazy to task in high style, suggesting that any show of indulgence is unwarranted: "[J]ust as
he is a poor soldier whose sole aim is to escape detention,
so he is a poor Christian whose sole aim is to escape Hell."
Auden, meanwhile, sends anger down some subtle byways:

"To speak of the Wrath of God cannot mean that God is Himself angry." Because the laws of the spiritual life are the very laws that define our nature, Auden suggests that we can defy but never break them. Should any souls wind up in hell, "it is not because they have been sent there, but because Hell is where they insist upon being."

Over the years other writers have sallied forth with varying success to confront the seven deadlies, usually with our best interests at heart. Unfortunately, the well-intentioned are more concerned with grace than with graceful prose, and their books will appeal only to the converted. The same, happily, cannot be said of the writers engaged in the new Oxford University Press series. Oxford has reprised Ian Fleming's project and taken it up a notch, commissioning seven slender volumes from seven contemporary scribes. True, it seems a publishing ploy on the order of forming a boy band, but there is precedent – although, as before, the pairing of writer and sin is not immediately evident.* Why would an Englishman be asked to write about lust, ponders Simon Blackburn. "Other nationalities are amazed that we English reproduce at all."

The trouble with sin nowadays is that there's no sting in the tale. Without a firm conviction of the soul's vertical passage, either up or down, sin is neutered, shorn of religious

---

* In order of publication we now have Joseph Epstein on *Envy*, Francine Prose on *Gluttony*, Simon Blackburn on *Lust*, Phyllis A. Tickle on *Greed*, Wendy Wasserstein on *Sloth*, Robert A. F. Thurman on *Anger*, and Michael Eric Dyson on *Pride*. The books grew out of lectures delivered at the New York Public Library, and the final results, slim as they are, still feel a bit padded, because a little sin does not go very far. The Brits were wise to keep them at essay length.

fear and loathing. Sin has to have some bite to it if it's going to make an impression on the page, which is not to say that the Oxford series is anything less than smart and civilized (and hence unpalatable to the sanctimonious who want their sins demonized). The authors, of course, recognize the dilemma of writing about sin for secularists. Gluttony, as Francine Prose observes, has become "an affront to prevailing standards of beauty and health rather than an offense against God." When sin has been co-opted by the helping professions, it should come as no surprise to learn that a congregation of French chefs recently petitioned the Vatican to remove gluttony from the list (though, apparently, it's more of a semantic dispute than a religious one).

It's probably fair to say that we've become desensitized to the word, if not the Word. In those secular neighborhoods where sin has been replaced by morality and "cultural norms," people don't fail God so much as they fail themselves and one another. And given the influence of early traumatic experience, genetic makeup, and our peripatetic hormones, the condemnation, if not morality, of certain behaviors becomes problematic. It's not sin that besets us, it's poor impulse control, selfishness, and depression. Chemistry *is* fate, up to a point; and lust and gluttony are joined at the lip. Does that not absolve the obese adulterer of sin if not of wrongdoing? Unless one is a true believer, sin is a conceit rather than something waiting to pounce and drive us straight into the ground.

The truth is, the concept of sin is not required to recognize contemptible and malignant behavior. Serious consequences, after all, attend certain acts whether we call them vices or sins. Is murder any less evil for being sinless? Hardly. God's law aside, there is some behavior whose maliciousness is sufficient to tie the perpetrator to the rack. Hell merely simplifies the question of punishment. Even among the religious, there was and remains disagreement regarding the exact nature of our transgressions. Whom and what are we to believe? Luther, for example, decreed that all the sins of unbelievers are mortal sins, and all the sins of the faithful, with the exception of infidelity, are venial. Yet one can go all of one's life without committing adultery, and grace, according to Luther, is still not guaranteed.

It is this unyielding moral absolutism that makes it possible to believe in God without taking the idea of sin too seriously. The momentous, the significant, fact of Creation is God, not man. On the other hand, if one is convinced that He sent His only begotten Son to save us, then the soul rather than Creation becomes the point. Got soul? Then you've got sin. Got soul, then you also have a body that houses it, and most of the cardinal sins, as we know, are associated with the body's unregulated appetites. If we were all purely spiritual entities, sin wouldn't be a problem. Nor, logically speaking, would Christianity. The point has been made before: Christianity is a religion of the body. The devout regard the body of Christ with unabashed fetishistic devotion (Mel Gibson's *Passion* does well to remind us of this), and although we can imaginatively divorce other religions from their founders – it didn't have to be Abraham per se or Mohammed or Buddha – we cannot accomplish this with Jesus. Christ is God; his arms, legs, tongue, and teeth are God.

All the same, the body is pretty loathsome – just ask Paul – and the distinction that is sometimes made between the "sins of the flesh" and the body does not really work. Bodies are flesh; divinity is not. God does not sneeze, nor does He bleed. But God did bleed when He took bodily form, and perhaps this helps explain the conflicting strains in Christianity regarding the sins. If God created the body in His image, should we not honor Him by using it to make ourselves happy? Well, that would depend on whom you ask. For most Christian theologians and lawgivers, separating the body from its trespasses and establishing what aspects of the body may be enjoyed without guilt are thorny issues. Just how much pleasure, if any, is allowed during procreation?

Sin, however we think of it, is always a struggle with our own bodies. But the body isn't all bad. It isn't just some physical impediment that we scale in order to reach God; it's the means of providing for consciousness. Unless one is an implacable idealist, it's obvious that the mind needs the body to teach it to become mind, and mind is the means by which we conceive God. Thank God, then, for the body. That said, our affinity to Him is found in our ability to think. If He made us, He made us to reason. And if He made us, He also made us imperfect (or the apple took care of that). And because we are imperfect, and because sin is pervasive, it's reasonable to assume that He wants us to become perfect by defeating sin. In effect, sin exists to make us worthy of Him. And the best way of showing that special affinity is to defeat sin through the gift He gave us – free will. We can therefore assume that He would want our devotion (if we can say that God "wants") to be a thoughtful devotion, for how much greater is faith when it comes through reason rather than from terror or insecurity or need of comfort? It's a struggle, of course, but as Augustine said, God wants us to struggle. It's why free will and evil both exist. Aquinas tends to agree: Evil is part of His plan and so it must be good. Indeed, it's what we must overcome to attain the supreme good that is God.

Let us forget for the moment the Church's rules for keeping souls in line or the prospect of incurring God's wrath (which Auden was correct in doubting); sin is a question of *wanting*. We want wealth, power, and status; we want this man's money and that man's wife; we want to win, we want revenge, we want to rest. And whenever we want too much, we want Him less. Sin is a question of *emphasis*: the grasping at earthly happiness instead of reaching toward heaven. One might even say that the essence of sin is the attempt to secure happiness instead of being willing to receive it. Since the gift of true happiness comes from God, any undue attempt to attain it on earth casts suspicion on His power to bestow it. Again, if God's essence is mind – rational, perfect, perpetual, and precise – we can realize Him only through mind; and if the mind is clouded, disturbed, or in thrall to earthly delights, we're in trouble. So it's also a question of *degree*. How much pleasure or distraction is too much? As Blackburn sensibly notes in *Lust*, "If we build the notion of excess into the definition, the desire is damned simply by its name." In other words, we can enjoy ourselves so long as enjoyment doesn't blot out God – not something most of us want to think about when spooning toward the bottom of a pint of Chunky Monkey or, for that matter, spooning with someone we like.

Ultimately, sin is a problem only for the sinful, which is another way of saying that the believer and the nonbeliever cannot shake hands across the spiritual divide. The secular not only reject the plausibility of sin; they may well wonder how anyone who really does believe in God *could* sin. I mean, there's hell to pay: twisting and turning in the fiery pit ... FOREVER! One would have to be an idiot to believe in sin and commit it too. But perhaps that's too simplistic. Perhaps the emphasis should not be on the sin but on the *temptation* to sin in the full knowledge that God exists. It's incorrect, then, to accuse Jimmy Swaggart and Jim Bakker of hypocrisy, or the hundreds of priests who abused young boys; that would mean they didn't believe. The truth is, they believed and they *still* couldn't help themselves, which is, in effect, the point: Without belief in the soul and the afterlife there is no sin. So who is more admirable: the virtuous who instinctively lead righteous lives, or the weak and easily tempted who put the lid on their lust or envy every waking moment? Isn't the alcoholic who refuses a drink more deserving of our respect than the teetotaler who thinks its morally wrong to knock back a beer?

On the whole, it helps to have sin around; it's like having a set of instructions for building a life that God approves of. We may have free will, but what are our choices when it comes to salvation? We can choose to do good or to do evil. Take away sin, however, and free will has no ballast, no epistemological basis of absolute moral certainty. Even if ethics is a "condition of the world, like logic," as Wittgenstein suggests, how in the world can it be demonstrated? Upon what blackboard would Wittgenstein have us look? What's a free moral agent to do?

The obvious answer is: keep looking for answers, keep weighing the effect of behavior against the desire that prompts it and the satisfaction gained when indulging it. It's not a simple equation, and, like school children, we have to struggle to balance the equation's parts. That's one way of looking at it. Another is to dismiss with prejudice the idea of original sin, discount the prospect of souls becoming muddier the longer their sojourn on earth, and instead concentrate on doing good because goodness makes sense. If everyone did good (like "obscenity" we know "goodness" when we see it), the world probably *would* make sense. But human nature being what it is, we may have to pull up a chair in society's emergency room and settle in for a long wait. Those tired of working on the equation can always turn to Paul. Me, I prefer to look to a blonder, more bosomy expositor of morals and ruefully concede: "To err is human – but it feels divine."

An African American
in
Regency England

THOMAS JEFFERSON, who could be quite stern on the subject of kings, could be equally stern about their amusements. In a 1785 letter, the future president cautioned that a young American who travels to England "learns drinking, horse racing, and boxing. . . . He acquires a fondness for European luxury and dissipation, and a contempt for the simplicity of his own country." As it happened, a young American who set sail for England some years later bore out Jefferson's dire prediction. But what Jefferson had not foreseen was that the young man would be a freed slave from Jefferson's own state of Virginia and that he would learn to box so well that he nearly brought down England's reigning champion.

Tom Molineaux's name is all but forgotten today, but in 1810 it was on the lips of everyone from the Prince of Wales and the young Lord Byron to the toughs and swells who made up the "fancy," the motley crew that followed sporting events. Boxing may not have been the sport of kings, but for a time it came close. Regulated bare-knuckle bouts, which had died out with the gladiatorial games, reappeared during the Restoration, attaining semiofficial recognition when a cudgel-and-sword instructor named James Figg appointed himself champion in 1719. Figg, whose broad, half-smiling face was captured by Hogarth, became the sport's first popularizer, and his exhibitions in a London amphitheater drew crowds that included the likes of Alexander Pope and Jonathan Swift.

43

Owing to the public brawling that prize fights occasioned, the sport was officially but ineffectively banned in 1750. In 1786 the Prince of Wales and his brother the Duke of York attended a fight between Richard Humphries and Sam "the Bath Butcher" Martin; and though the prince's enthusiasm for "milling," as boxing was then called, soon waned, the fashion had been set. Other dukes, earls, and lesser nobles began sponsoring likely prospects, encouraged by a new and better class of skilled pugilists including the spry Jem Belcher; the future M.P. John Gully; "Gentleman" John Jackson; the counterpuncher Daniel Mendoza, a Sephardic Jew whose memoirs claim a long conversation with George III ("who made many ingenious remarks on the pugilistic art"); and the indomitable Tom Cribb, whose two fights with Molineaux in 1810 and 1811 galvanized not only the sporting world but much of Great Britain as well.

Boxing wasn't just big in Britain around the time of the Regency, it *was* British – British because it was humanitarian (bouts had replaced duels), because it was egalitarian (aficionados cut across all levels of society), and because it embodied the cultural ethos of manliness and fair play. But mainly boxing was British because no other nation seemed in a hurry to take it up. "Foreigners can scarcely understand how we can squeeze pleasure out of this pastime," Hazlitt wrote a bit smugly. Indeed, they could not. But on the scepter'd isle, the seat of Mars, the pleasure taken in fisticuffs had a distinct jingoist flavor. With Napoleon rolling across Europe and the Battle of Trafalgar still fresh in the public mind, most Britons tended to equate the mettle demonstrated in the prize ring with the courage demanded

on the battlefield. "Never did I see such a pounding match," Wellington said of Waterloo a month after the battle. "Both [armies] were what the boxers call gluttons." The English may have been "a nation of shopkeepers," but they were damned tough shopkeepers – Tom Cribb the toughest of them all.

Tom Molineaux's startling appearance in London, then, must have seemed like the prank of some Anglophobic genie. Not only was Molineaux a Negro, he was an *American* Negro. Not only did he have the effrontery to challenge the champion – a man justly admired for his skills and renowned for his fighting heart – he had the gall to predict victory. After handily defeating two opponents, Molineaux strutted around the West End, openly boasting of the damage he'd inflict on the champion once they squared off. Bad form indeed. But, more important, Molineaux's behavior and ambition flew in the face of prevailing racial and pugilistic assumptions. A black man challenging for the title? And an American to boot? Well, it simply defied the natural order. It was as if a tallish citizen of Baghdad had deplaned in Chicago in 1999 and proceeded to taunt Michael Jordan, demanding he play him one-on-one.

In short, Molineaux was sport's first authentic bête noire: a flamboyant, overbearing, self-aggrandizing black athlete, whose posturing aroused such widespread anxiety that for a time his fights even overshadowed the war with Napoleon. To the English, and probably even to those who sympathized with the plight of the Negro, he was insupportable. Thank God, then, for Tom Cribb. "Of the whole race of pugilists, no boxer was ever considered *safer* to back," declared Pierce Egan, the first chronicler of the London Prize Ring. Nevertheless, "the *tremendous* man of *colour*" did look formidable, and what if, God forbid, he were to win? "It appeared somewhat as a national concern," Egan would recall. "ALL felt for the honor of their country."

45

The danger to the national honor actually had its roots in America years before Molineaux arrived on the scene. In 1763 a child was born on Staten Island to a black mother and white father. The boy's name was Bill Richmond. When Richmond was thirteen he was taken to England by General Lord Percy, the future second Duke of Northumberland. Lord Percy taught Richmond to read and write and later had him apprenticed to a carpenter. Richmond, however, had other ideas. An excellent athlete, he took up cricket and boxing, and in short order became England's first black sportsman. In 1805, when Richmond was forty-two, he lasted an hour and a half against a younger and stronger Cribb, for whom he conceived a strong dislike. Despite this loss, Richmond did well for himself. He saved his money, opened a public house, and started a boxing academy where he taught the gentry the finer points of milling.

Because everyone knew Richmond, it was only natural that another black pugilist would be steered his way. An odd meeting it must have been: the educated property owner whose character was praised by both Egan and Hazlitt, and the boisterous, illiterate newcomer whom most people apparently found hard to stomach. Richmond probably disliked him, too, but he also realized that Molineaux was the genuine article, an opportunity not only to best Cribb but to raise a black man to England's most coveted sporting title. By the time Richmond arranged for Cribb to meet his protégé, the buzz was tremendous. There had been anticipated contests before – but none like this. Cribb vs. Molineaux was the first great sporting event of the modern era, the one fight that everyone who was anyone had to attend.

46   On a wet and blustery day in December of 1810, ten thousand spectators gathered on Copthall Common, Sussex, to watch Tom Cribb defend his title. The battle, which lasted fifty-five minutes and thirty-four rounds (rounds were measured by falls, not by minute intervals) was terrific. Although the twenty-nine-year-old Cribb came in fat (he did not take Molineaux very seriously), betting was heavily in favor of the champion. An expert miller, the cognoscenti will tell you, requires not only patience and discipline but a cool head, which puts mastery out of the reach of lazy, hot-tempered foreigners. Molineaux, however, was unaware of this. He began strong and became stronger, and by the sixth round no bets were being offered on Cribb. At the end of the tenth round, both men were down. Despite vicious counterpunching by Cribb, Molineaux bored in. By round fourteen, the odds began to favor Molineaux. Cribb now began to tire, but in the fifteenth round he caught Molineaux with a punch to the throat. Molineaux went down, then rallied. In the nineteenth round, Cribb was forced against the ropes, which gave spectators a chance to grab Molineaux's hand in order to break his fingers; they may have succeeded. Molineaux plugged away and dropped Cribb in rounds twenty and twenty-one. After the twenty-eighth round (the number remains in dispute), Cribb seemed done for, unable to rise at the call of "Time."

It was at this point, Egan reports, that Cribb's second, Joe Ward, "by a little maneuvering, occupied the attention of the Black's seconds, and so managed to prolong the period sufficiently to enable the champion to recover a little, and thus assist him to pull through." The truth is a bit more damning. When Ward saw that Cribb was out on his feet, he rushed across the ring and accused Richmond of having placed two bullets in Molineaux's fists (a trick to make the blows heavier). No bullets were found, but the ensuing confusion gave Cribb precious seconds to recover. The fight resumed, but Molineaux was demoralized. His defense collapsed; he suffered chills and was unable to come to scratch after the thirty-fourth round.

For the record, Molineaux lost. Those who saw the fight, however, knew better. The Prince of Wales himself, it is said, remarked that Molineaux had won, and certainly Cribb knew that his victory was tainted. More important, London's black population, which then numbered between twelve and fifteen thousand souls, must have derived a great deal of satisfaction from Molineaux's performance. Although people of color were confined to a marginal existence as grooms and servants and were often employed without pay, they formed a distinct community, with established lines of communication. They may not have been present at Copthall Common that day, but they must have heard, as Egan would later write, that "the Black astonished everyone not only by his extraordinary power of hitting, and his gigantic strength, but also by his acquaintance with the science, which was far greater than any had given him credit for."

And that, of course, was the reason that Molineaux had been allowed to challenge for the title in the first place. No one expected a black man to know the finer points of boxing or to stand up against Cribb (Richmond, an honorary Englishman, being the exception). When Molineaux stepped into the ring, no groundswell of disapproval rose to greet him. He was allowed to fight; he was just not allowed to win. Only after Molineaux's death did Egan concede: "It will not be forgotten, if justice holds the scales, that his *colour* alone prevented him from becoming the hero of that fight;

at the same time, it is due to *Cribb* to observe, that he was in very bad condition."

48   A week or so after the contest, a letter addressed to "Mr. Thomas Cribb, St. Martin's Street, Leicester Square, December 21, 1810," appeared in the London papers:

> Sir, – My friends think that had the weather on last Tuesday, the day on which I contended with you, not been so unfavourable, I should have won the battle; I therefore challenge you to a second meeting, at any time within two months, for such a sum as those gentlemen who place confidence in me may be pleased to arrange.
>
> As it is possible this letter may meet the public eye, I cannot omit the opportunity of expressing a confident hope, that the circumstances of my being of a different colour to that of a people amongst whom I have sought protection, will not in any way operate to my prejudice.
>
> I am, sir,
> Your most obedient humble servant
> T. MOLINEAUX

The challenge, most likely penned by Egan, is a small masterpiece, effectively playing to the Britons' vaunted sense of fair play. The inclement weather is, of course, code for the injustice Molineaux suffered in the later rounds; and by mentioning his color and his dependence on the English, the letter left Cribb little choice in the matter.

This time Cribb trained. He put himself in the hands of Robert Barclay Allardice, better known as "Captain Barclay," a famous exercise nut and "pedestrian" (he walked long distances in quick time), who pelted Cribb's shins with pebbles until the irritated champion took after him. Apparently, Barclay ran him silly. Molineaux, on the other hand, inexplicably disdained the rigors of training, preferring to spend his nights in "flash houses" among thieves and prostitutes.

The rematch, held on September 28, 1811, at Thistleton Gap, outside London, was even more anxiously anticipated than the first Cribb–Molineaux match. Twenty thousand spectators jostled to get a view, and of these, Egan estimated, a quarter were of "the highest mould, including some of the principal Corinthians of the State." But Molineaux was in no shape to withstand Cribb's onslaught. He fought gamely, but Cribb was in trim fighting condition and delivered a fearsome beating. The contest was over in nineteen minutes. England celebrated; Molineaux convalesced.

Afterward, Molineaux – none the worse for wear – took to the road, fighting and staging exhibitions, while continuing to drink and carouse. Richmond finally washed his hands of him, dunned him for money, and even seconded one of his opponents. It didn't matter; restraint and common sense were foreign to Molineaux. On reflection, he seems like the modern ur-athlete, as unpredictable and self-destructive as any newly minted millionaire fresh out of college or high school – more a prophecy of things to come than a mere precursor. By 1818, he was battered and spent. Exhausted and fever ridden, he died in a barn in Galway, attended by two soldiers of the 77th Foot. He was thirty-four years old.

How has such a story escaped the attention of all but a few historians of popular culture? Why haven't more academicians, especially in these racially sensitive times, picked up Molineaux's trail? There are, of course, good reasons for the absence of accurate biographical material. For one thing, boxing history is not history writ with a capital H; for another, Molineaux's name was bruited at a time when boxing in America was not established. American newspapers barely deigned to notice a former slave, even neglecting to tweak the British with his prowess. The *New York Evening Post* (February 18, 1811), for example, simply copied, without comment, a round-by-round description of the rematch from an English journal. More surprisingly, the first American history of prizefighting – *American Fistiana*, compiled in 1849 – somehow managed to omit his name.

Because literally everything that we know about Molineaux has been culled from British sources, in particular Egan's classic five-volume *Boxiana, or Sketches of Ancient and Modern Pugilism* (1812), which arose out of the tremendous interest generated by the Cribb–Molineaux fights, no one seems able to account for how Molineaux came to England. Neither Jonathan Badcock's *The Fancy, or True Sportsman's Guide by an Operator* (1826) nor Henry Downes Miles's *Pugilistica* (1863) offers a glimpse of Molineaux's first twenty-five years in America. Nathaniel Fleischer's unreliable *Black Dynamite* (New York, 1938) has Molineaux born in Washington, D.C., but other sources have him born in Maryland or Virginia. According to Fleischer, Molineaux came from a boxing family (extremely unlikely) and was manumitted by his owner in Virginia after he beat another slave in a matched fight (also unlikely). Frederick W. J. Henning's *Fights for the Championship* (London, 1903) postulates that a British sailor named Davis, after seeing Molineaux fight on the New York docks, was responsible for bringing him to England. But the facts are spotty and difficult to verify.

A more complete but decidedly more imaginary history

is to be found in George MacDonald Fraser's novel *Black Ajax* (1997). Fraser plants the young Molineaux in Louisiana (the French name being a hint of his origins) and goes on to create a ribald and unappetizing portrait of the man. Unapologetically dishing up the racial argot of the day, Fraser gives us a highly entertaining, always informative, and even sympathetic view of a black man in nineteenth-century London. Certainly no other novel better conveys the heightened wartime atmosphere of Regency England or the significance of the London Prize Ring. The Regency may have begun in 1811, but, as one character growls, "Who cares for that when the Championship of England was at stake, with black hands clutching at Britannia's crown?"

Admittedly, a few American historians have recently taken account of Molineaux's existence, but all draw heavily on Paul Magriel's "Tom Molineaux: Career of an American Negro Boxer in England and Ireland," a patchwork essay that appeared in *Phylon: the Atlanta University Review of Race and Culture* (December 1951). Elliot Gorn's excellent *The Manly Art* (1986) devotes half a dozen pages to Molineaux's travails in England with the advisement that "the most astonishing thing about Tom Molineaux is that we know so little about him"; and Gerald Early's *The Culture of Bruising* (1994) contains a moving if somewhat embarrassing tribute to him. To this day, bibliographies of prominent African Americans contain only one to five listings for him

Molineaux, of course, left no letters or journals. Nevertheless, historical context does suggest probable causes for his behavior. That he popped up in England in 1809 is not in itself surprising. If he had worked and fought on the New York docks, then he would have run into British sailors and heard of the London Prize Ring. He might also have heard that blacks in England were generally better off than their freed counterparts in the States. Quite probably, he arrived in London full of hope and determination; and very likely, he soon met with shock and disappointment. This was a world in which a prince of the realm might shake his hand and wish him luck, while a spectator at a fight could call out "Huzzah for the nigger" without thinking it an insult. And when "nigger" is not meant as an insult, it may speak to a deeper and more penetrating prejudice.

52

Although many Britons felt that slavery was invidious, few actually believed that Africans were equal to whites. Even most abolitionists believed in the natural inferiority of the African, in his inherent childishness and simplicity – assumptions so ingrained as to be axiomatic. Such prejudice is not benign (it even depends on the seeming complicity of blacks to sustain it), yet may afford opportunities for advancement precluded by *outright* bias. For it was only when racial assumptions began to be undermined, when prejudice became fueled by the secret fear that perhaps blacks *were* equal to whites, that whites actively undertook to keep every black person down, especially those who displayed talent. In 1908, Jack Johnson was hindered from fighting a title bout not only because he was black, but because it was felt he could win; and in 1947 Jackie Robinson was reviled not only because of his race, but because he could play a damn sight better than most whites.

It was, of course, prejudice beyond any shadow of doubt, beyond any anxiety over its rightness, that puts Molineaux's astonishing life in perspective. Although Egan appreciated his "towering and restless ambition . . . [which] induced him to quit his home and country and erect his hostile standard among the British heroes," these words cannot convey what awaited him. Molineaux fought for the title a full century before Jack Johnson finally chased down Tommy Burns in Australia. What he must have felt and what he was made to feel can scarcely be imagined today.

Any characterization of Molineaux is perforce colored – hardly a pun in this case – by those who drew or described him. "The *Black* naturally had a taste for gaiety," Egan observed, "a strong passion for dress – was amorously inclined, and full of gallantry. With *togs* of the best quality and fashion, the *Man of Colour* soon appeared as a *blade* of the first magnitude." Who this blade really was, we may never know. We know only what his contemporaries observed or thought they observed. Egan, who liked him, still made sport of him; and one has only to glance at the caricatures by Thomas Rowlandson or George and Robert Cruikshank to be struck by the exaggerated Negroid (i.e., "savage") features of Molineaux's face.

Perhaps Molineaux did squander his money, talent, and health; perhaps he *was* brash and arrogant and liked riding into a new town in a post chaise and four, pulling up at the best inn, and partying all night. On the other hand, his outrageous behavior could have been a means of creating interest in his fights. Or in himself. Molineaux's antics, as Egan notes, "had the desired effect in bringing numbers to witness his sparring exhibitions." If you thought Cassius Clay was mouthing poetry because he wanted the editors of the Yale Younger Poets Series to admire him, you were mistaken.

Of one thing, at least, we can be certain: however Molineaux was greeted and treated, it was never as an equal. And perhaps it was this, and not the injustice of that fateful later round in the first championship fight, that made him self-destruct. There is, after all, a poignant mystery at the heart of the story. Molineaux did not train for the rematch and by not training ensured his own defeat. Had he won, he would have been champion of England. In truth, win or lose, he could have had a good life. If he had behaved, he could have gained the backing of a patron and become rich — but he chose not to. He chose to sneer at the fancy and he chose ruin over a good reputation. Why? It's hard to say. Perhaps he knew that he was not cut from the same cloth as Richmond and that he would always be seen as an American nigger. But bowing to his detractors was not in his nature, and to be accepted as a dog that doesn't bite is no acceptance at all. So he threw society's offer, his chance at respectability, back in its face, and proceeded to shorten his own life as quickly and as furiously as he could. In rejecting civilized conduct, he rejected the civilization that maintained the institution of slavery until 1833. Of all that Egan wrote about him, perhaps the truest words were these: "Notwithstanding his alleged ferocity, he laboured under considerable depression."

In 1821, the Prince Regent ascended to the throne. Those attending the coronation of George IV may have noticed some twenty rough-looking men dressed as royal pages. These were the honor guard: England's finest boxers. Cribb was there, of course, as were Bill Richmond, John Jackson, and John Gully. It was pugilism's own crowning moment. One likes to think that Molineaux would have sent his regrets.

Hello,
Beautiful

Beauty is a mess, a sinkhole, a trap. Approach it philosophically and you're immediately bogged down in questions of idealism, empiricism, subjectivity, and objectivity. Plato began the conversation; Kant tried to finish it; and Santayana, embracing Plato and Kant, tried to encapsulate it. Take a cultural run at it, and you're stumbling over issues of relativism, where nothing is either beautiful or ugly, but time, class, nation, or ethnicity makes it so. There is also everything that artists, poets, and critics have said about beauty, with enough variance in emphasis to make your head spin. More recently, an entirely new field of study has emerged that considers beauty – and attendant feelings of attraction and repulsion – from an evolutionary standpoint. And, as if all this were not enough, there exists the impression that no matter what or how much is said about beauty, something is sure to remain unsaid.

Such an eventuality, however, did not deter Umberto Eco from running to meet it. His *History of Beauty* is both grand and companionable, mixing erudition and philosophical sophistication with contemporary notions of the cool and the fashionable.* Beauty – needless to say – cannot be scissioned from the media and the movies, but Eco perhaps bends too far to accommodate fashion. We understand that the publisher would like the book to sell, and we take some pleasure in the fact that Dennis Rodman's dream of sharing a book with Denis Diderot has finally been realized, but any history of ideas that refers to "the refined masculine Beauty of Richard Gere" tends to weaken its scholarly pedigree. Eco, on occasion, gives the impression of wanting to be a Hegelian hipster, which is a little like wanting to see the Parthenon tap dance, but it's a small enough failing in a book that tackles such a dizzying and capacious subject.

Before beauty gets stuck in the eye of the beholder, it must first exist elsewhere. Before it's an idea, it's a sensation, which the mind transforms into a recognizable experience. That experience is pleasure, and though pleasure is particular, the expectation of it presumably is common to all. Disagreeing about what is or isn't beautiful doesn't discredit the notion of beauty; it simply aims a word at a number of different targets. The targets change, but the concept remains. "At what point," T. S. Eliot wondered, "does the attempt to design and create an object for the sake of beauty become conscious? At what point in civilization does any conscious distinction between practical or magical utility and aesthetic beauty arise?" Eliot is reminding us that Neolithic cave paintings, Sumerian seals, and Egyptian sarcophagus carvings were not created to be "beautiful," nor was the response to them an aesthetic one, at least not in the way we use the word.†

---

* American edition, Rizzoli International Publications, Inc., 2004.

† Aesthetics (from the Greek *aisthetikos*, or "perceptual") was first used in 1750 to designate a theory of "sensuous cognition" by the German

Aesthetic beauty began with Plato, who, with a nod toward Pythagoras, elevated the term *kalos* – which Homer had applied to pleasing or sensuous appearance – into an immutable Form or Ideal. The Beautiful reconciled the universal with the particular and manifested itself in proportion, harmony, and due measure. Anything said to be "beautiful" thus participated in the idea of beauty, which, like Goodness and Truth, was eternal. Aristotle accepted beauty's essential otherworldliness but also allowed for differences, stressing, for instance, beauty's concrete realization in art.

By the time the idea of beauty entered the mainstream of Western thought through the writings of Plotinus and Augustine, it had become a creative force, identified with the cosmos itself. As the expression of God's will, the cosmos (which means "order") was necessarily and ineluctably beautiful. The Middle Ages may have had its wars and pestilences, but these were only temporal disruptions. Perfection and eternity awaited, augured in the sublunar world by harmony and regularity. Indeed, the more regular an object's configuration, the more beautiful it was. An equilateral triangle, according to Augustine, was more beautiful than a scalene one; a square more beautiful than a triangle; a circle more beautiful still; and the point, which is its own center and from which all points flow, was the most beautiful object of all. But Beauty, so to speak, was not the point. In God's *harmonium mundi*, Reason explained everything, from the insects on the ground to the spheres in the heavens.

The conversation begun by Plato was now being engaged by those who believed that God was listening – in which case art could not help but do the bidding of religion. And those charged with the creation of beauty, though they may

thinker Alexander Baumgarten, who proposed to establish a science of the beautiful.

have argued over technique, were not "artists" or arbiters of taste, but artisans who understood that the classical rules of order also reflected God's order.* Therefore a cathedral, in the words of the medievalist historian Henri Focillon, was "a considered arrangement of symmetries and repetitions, a law of numbers, a kind of music of symbols silently co-ordinating these vast encyclopedias of stone." With God in the details, it was only natural to spy the abstract in the sensuous, or the Platonic in the Aristotelian. And since God intended that we recognize Him by His works, St. Thomas Aquinas could infer that beauty was equivalent to integrity or perfection, due proportion and *claritas*.

Generally speaking, the history of philosophy is a wavering narrative of increased subjectivity, of moving from the object of thought to thoughts about the object. From Descartes on, philosophy has, in one form or another, addressed the irrefutable dualism of existence – of being and thinking about being – which pretty much denies the possibility of an absolute answer, unless, of course, God provides. But once God leaves the building, on what philosophical foundation does the building rest? From what window is beauty to be viewed?

The process of easing beauty from its theological perch began during the Renaissance in Italy with the efflorescence of painting and sculpture, the rise of literary criticism, and the increasingly independent status of the artisan as artist. As art gained legitimacy, divesting itself of religious and

---

* Even the ancient Greeks (who did not know Him) made the space between columns of temples, or between parts of the façade, correspond to the same ratios that govern musical intervals, since such proportions signified the reason that filled the universe.

teleological instruction, beauty changed from being a property of the Ideal to being an attribute of the real. Classical
rules still applied to artistic expression, but a subtle shift was
occurring. The Copernican revolution, which had thrown
the earth into orbit around the sun, also shifted man's interests from divine workings to his own more perishable
works. Although this was no small readjustment, it was
Johannes Kepler's revelation – as Eco nicely points out –
that resonated with artists. Copernicus may have moved
the center of the universe, but it was Kepler who discov-
ered that "celestial bodies do not follow simple Classical
harmonies, but require a steadily growing complexity."

59

Now arguments about art and beauty could *really* begin.
If appearances were not what they seemed, then the mirror
that artists held up to nature had to do more than reflect
what it faced.* The Enlightenment, which was about many
things, was also about man's ability to explain, rather than
merely intuit, the universal principles that govern perception. God still presided, but He did not necessarily assist.
One therefore did not slight Divinity by questioning the
relationship between the beautiful and the qualities Aquinas
ascribed to it. Perhaps man himself had a say in what was
beautiful and what wasn't.

So beauty became fair game for anyone who desired to
produce it or think about its meaning. The Greeks may have
invented the Beautiful, but they also narrowed its meaning by placing it in the empyrean realm. (You can limit
ideas by making them eternal.) It was the Enlightenment

---

* This concern ran through the seventeenth-century *querelle des anci-
ennes et des modernes*, which pitted writers who favored innovation in
the arts against those who insisted on maintaining long-established rules
of decorum. For the "moderns," a work could be beautiful without hewing to the classical verities of symmetry, harmony, and clarity.

philosophers who worried at beauty, who, in fact, brought it down to earth. According to *The Eighteenth-Century Short Title Catalogue*, the word "beauty" appears 450 times, and "beautiful" 511 times. The most important title from a purely philosophical standpoint was Kant's *Critique of Judgment* (1790), although it took David Hume's essay "Of the Standard of Taste," and Edmund Burke's *A Philosophical Inquiry into the Origins of our Ideas of the Sublime and Beautiful*, both published in 1757, to make aesthetic conundrums public.

For Hume, beauty, while relying on formal relationships, was not inherent in things themselves. Instead, things become beautiful insofar as the sensations associated with them please us because of nature, custom, or caprice. Since beauty depends on the mind that experiences it, experience serves to heighten our awareness and temper our judgments. Eventually, familiarity breeds "disinterestedness," and the pleasure consists of understanding how an object's construction and purpose fit together.

This is all well and good, but in what sense can such lofty appreciation be seen as truly valid? It can't. Indeed, in Hume's universe, nothing is certain beyond all logical doubt, which is the reason that Kant proposed a qualified subjectivism that could, at the same time, render absolute judgments. Although Kant conceded that disinterested pleasure was independent of inviolable rules or concepts, he somehow managed to convince himself that disinterested beauty was both universal and a "symbol of the morally good."

Edmund Burke, however, was not so sanguine. Following Hume's lead that sensations are at the root of whatever imperfect knowledge we may have, Burke also maintained that certain sensations, if powerful enough, are absolute in a way that brooks no disinterestedness. Beauty, apparently, "belongs" to things only when they induce in us feelings like "affection and tenderness." The qualities of objects that summon such feelings include comparative smallness, smoothness, variety (though the parts must be in some relation), and delicacy. So an Arabian horse wins out over a charger, and a greyhound over a mastiff. And a woman's beauty, incidentally, "is enhanced by [her] timidity, a quality of mind analogous to it." Is that a problem for anyone?

But beauty doesn't hold a candle to the sublime; in fact, it *is* a candle when compared to the sublime. Even more than Hume, Burke stressed the physiological effects of things. Beauty, for instance, which is characterized by charm, harmony, simplicity, radiance, along with perfection of detail, derives from feelings of pleasure and has a relaxing effect on the "fibers" of the human body. By contrast, the sublime, which derives from feelings of pain, tightens these fibers. Thus, the sublime in the form of a raging storm, a high mountain range, or a turbulent ocean cannot help but generate feelings of awe and astonishment, mingled with a dollop of fear. Beauty merely invites; the sublime commands.

By relegating beauty to what pleases us, Burke not only cut out its metaphysical heart but demoted it to mere appearances. Even the idea that the beautiful was composed – in both senses of the word, having form and serenity – worked to diminish it. The sublime, after all, was not so much composed as intimidating. One could turn away from beauty (since it depends on our apprehension of it) but not from the sublime, which exists independently of us. The effect of Burke's treatise was electric. If feeling rather than reason was behind artistic expression – if the sublime scattered pleasure and beauty before it, just as genius sent taste and the rules of decorum packing – then artists who demonstrated greater energy and raw power were better than the those who adhered to order and regularity. Because the beautiful could be realized, it was limited. But the sublime, which channeled the infinite and the inexpressible, could never be fully or artfully rendered. From this, Burke deduces that "a clear idea is therefore another name for a little idea." Goodbye, Aquinas and Descartes: with a wave of the sublime, Burke cast out the neoclassical.

By the end of the nineteenth century, whatever philosophical revisions and refinements the idea of beauty now accrued were but variations on a theme. What did change, of course, were attitudes toward beauty. The French Symbolist poets, for example, rapturously advocated a nuanced, allusive, and oblique form of beauty found in music and in the poetry that aspired to music. ("*Je suis belle, ô mortels! comme un rêve de pierre,*" wrote Baudelaire, in one of the loveliest and most mysterious lines in French poetry.) So rarified was this sense of artistic beauty that inevitably it came to be seen as superior to the more obvious charms offered by nature. "Nature has had her day ... [she has] exhausted the patience of refined temperaments," muses Des Esseintes, the protagonist of J-K Huysmans's 1884 *A Rebours*, a novel best read before the age of twenty-five. Yet Oscar Wilde loved it so much that he simply stole from it: "What Art really reveals to us is Nature's lack of design." Nature, Wilde wrote coyly, could not compete with art, and so a beautiful sunset became, in his estimation, only "a very second-rate Turner." Wilde, who was more playful than the French, was also more serious, though he could sometimes exaggerate to such a degree that one might miss his meaning entirely: "To discern the beauty of a thing is the finest point to which we can arrive. Even a color-sense is more important, in the development of the individual, than a sense of right and wrong." This might seem the axiom of a bona fide decadent, but Wilde, in truth, was almost naïve in his hopes for art, believing that if people were educated aesthetically, the ills of the world would disappear.*

The point of beauty's apex and the point of its steepest decline followed one another in rapid succession. The notorious 1910 and 1912 exhibitions of Post-Impressionist paintings in London, which introduced art that made undue demands on the audience, did not summarily push beauty aside; if the new art looked odd or unfamiliar, it was because, one didn't see the rationale behind the work or the unity that informed it. According to the curator Roger Fry, one had to know how to look; otherwise a truly original painting might be considered "ugly until it was seen as beautiful."

It was but a short step from Fry's intellectualization of artistic pleasure to Duchamp's *Fountain*. Disillusioned by the futility and senseless carnage of World War I, the first generation of the avant-garde rejected whatever moral values had made such a war possible and abandoned the idea of a metaphysic underlying artistic production. Genius was necessary, and a cold eye; but beauty and goodness – no. Such foolishness had nothing to do with reality or aesthetics.

This represents, of course, a rather hasty and reductive survey of twenty-five hundred years of critical discourse. Short of a book like Eco's *History of Beauty*, which contains scores of quotes pulled from just about everyone who had something to say on the subject, it's impossible to summarize the shadings and shifting emphases that have transformed beauty over the course of time. But it is possible to

---

* Anyone who wants to say anything at all about art or beauty would do well to consult Wilde's "The Decay of Lying" and "The Critic as Artist," which, albeit brief, contain multitudes.

identify a moment when beauty stopped being regarded as meaningful. Although Flaubert suggested in 1852 that "the time for beauty is over," he did not dismiss the aesthetic ideals that had dominated the literary and plastic arts since the Renaissance.* It remained for the avant-garde to do that. By 1948, when Barnett Newman got around to indicting beauty as the "bugbear of European art and European aesthetic philosophies," the aesthetic manifesto had long been edited to remove all traces of beauty's moral and philosophical significance.

It was only a matter of time, then, before critics and educators began to question beauty's role in civilization itself. An element of poststructuralist thought holds that beauty is nothing more than a cultural house of cards set up by the economically and educationally advantaged to reinforce the social hierarchy – a charge that has some merit, but not enough to demonstrate beauty's absence. But this trend, too, seems to have passed. As I write, beauty is back in the academy's good graces, and over the past ten years there have been scores of books and journal articles, as well as various symposia, devoted to the subject.[†]

Which is not to say that the professors are all in agreement. One of the reasons that any discussion of beauty soon

---

* Flaubert didn't repudiate beauty; he simply thought that chasing after it would get us nowhere. Instead, he urged that art and science work together to improve mankind.

[†] The trend began in 1995 with David Hickey's much praised but philosophically slippery *The Invisible Dragon: Four Essays on Beauty*, which argues for the reinstatement of pleasure in art. See also: Jeremy Gilbert-Role's *Beauty and the Contemporary Sublime*; Bill Beckley with David Shapiro's (eds.), *Uncontrollable Beauty*; Peter Schjeldahl's article "Beauty Is Back" in the *New York Times Magazine* (September 28, 1996); Elaine Scary's *On Beauty*; Wendy Steiner's *Venus in Exile*; and Denis Donoghue's *Speaking of Beauty*.

becomes troublesome is the intrusion and interaction of knowledge and memory. For instance, do we accord the same degree of beauty to a rug painstakingly made by a person over the course of nine months as to an *exact* duplicate produced by a machine in nine hours? Do rarity and monetary value affect the idea of beauty? And what about the role that affection plays? Many parents think their infant children beautiful, even if they happen to resemble small fish with beaks; and last year a poll in England disclosed that the most beautiful word in the English language was "mother." A nice sentiment, but a silly answer. A far better response, so a story goes, was proffered a half century ago by an Italian immigrant to these shores. When asked what he thought was the most beautiful word in the English language, he replied, "Cellar door."

The great aesthetic lesson of the twentieth century was that we could have art without beauty. Anyone could make something beautiful, but only a genius could make ART. A child, after all, might draw a line or put a daub of color on canvas and create beauty, but is that art? Hence, the problematic role of beauty in art is a peculiarly modern one – or, more accurately, a modernist one – created by the writers and artists who came of age around 1920 and who refused to cede intellectual rigor to aesthetic clarity. Whereas a certain recognizable combination of style and technical innovation was once generally accepted (fashion permitting) as constituting successful poems, paintings, and musical compositions, something new had been added to the mix: mainly, the complex interplay between artistic self-awareness and the difficulties involved in reinventing the various artistic genres. This is not to suggest that art before 1920 was more simple but that the nature of the complexity had changed. The appreciation of modernist works required a whole new set of critical tools.

Differentiating between art and beauty can be a messy business. Great works do not necessarily convey beauty in a similar manner, and sometimes a poem or painting's subject may disqualify it from rehearsing the usual notions of beauty. Art is not art because it succeeds in meeting the artist's or the critic's standards; something else is required, and it is not easy to pin down. It is beauty and, to state the obvious, there are variations of beauty in art. The lovely metrical touches of Herrick cannot be confused with the lyrical ceremoniousness of Yeats; and the tone poems of Debussy will not remind anyone of the *St. Matthew Passion*. But any attempt to measure and compare such respective beauties is absurd. Nor, for that matter, can we restrict the recognition of beauty to those best qualified to judge art.

Not that I wish to appear democratic or open minded, but the people swaying to the pedestrian lyrics and repetitive harmonics at a John Tesh concert are, by their lights, experiencing beauty. One look at their adoring faces is all the proof we need. By the same token, a man eating a hot dog on the street might be enjoying himself as much as a gourmand savoring a slice of duck breast at Taillevent. That said, one can also say that aesthetic sophistication increases one's chances of encountering beauty; it creates the possibility of *more*, if not more intense, experiences of the beautiful. To be aware of the intricacies of dance, the degree of difficulty in writing poetry, the notes and tempo involved in music, is to appreciate what may not be *immediately* apparent – in which case pleasure takes on a new dimension.

There is no shame in confessing that part of the pleasure we derive from modern art is the satisfaction of "understanding" it. Pleasure, of course, is a loaded term, but not one we can ignore. It is, after all, what first draws us to art. The sensible George Santayana observed that beauty begins with sensation: what we like immediately, and especially what we like as children, is the best proof of sincerity. And when "sincerity is lost, and a snobbish ambition is substituted, bad taste comes in." But so does ambiguity. Standards of taste cannot be limited to what is immediately apparent. Hume understood this when he proposed the "disinterestedness" that comes from experience. At some point, if one makes a fetish of art, the appeal of immediacy wanes, and artworks become aesthetically significant rather than beautiful. And from this it's a quick tumble into a cultural relativism where aesthetic evaluation and class-bound values become entangled.

Cultural materialists might argue that bias is always a factor when judging something or someone beautiful. I tend to agree. But just as some people can put social prejudices behind them, others are better able to see both art and beauty for what they are in purely aesthetic terms. The counterargument here is that aesthetics itself is culturally determined. But you know what? It isn't, or at least not entirely. Not everyone is so easily shaped by his or her environment. There are, I believe, people temperamentally predisposed to value beauty apart from the culture's valuations of it. (Wilde even thought we have a "beauty-sense.") Beauty is *both* a custom and a longing, and some people require beauty more than others; they may even feel that it's their life's work. The reason is simple: beauty has an existence apart from an individual's emotional attachment to people or things. Stendhal, who wrote the book *On Love*, put it baldly: "It may be that men who are not susceptible to passion are those who feel the effect of beauty most." What a cold and extraordinary notion – yet there is truth to it. To appreciate beauty in matters of art, as well as of the heart, requires a certain detachment. To love something for itself alone, for its formal components, is the mark of the true critic. So we return, yet again, to the eighteenth-century idea of disinterestedness. Wilde also touched on this, but more gently, when he suggested that "the only beautiful things, as somebody once said, are the things that do not concern us."

68   The "beauty-sense" divined by Wilde is not exactly what researchers in the field of evolutionary aesthetics have in mind when examining our attraction to, or repulsion from, sensory stimuli. Not content to regard beauty as a synthetic idea that simply differentiates between things that please or displease us, an interdisciplinary batch of thinkers have arisen who identify basic aesthetic preferences that, as a matter of Darwinian adaptability, cause us to be attracted to certain shapes and sounds as opposed to others. In sum, the argument is as follows: Whatever helped the first humans to survive must have appealed to them, and this knowledge of what was beneficial was programmed into their brains and inherited by subsequent generations. Our aesthetic preferences, therefore, are the result of evolved perceptual and cognitive abilities, and although the pleasure associated with them is no longer essential for survival, it continues to influence how we feel about both art and nature. Wilde may have had it backwards: beauty is *precisely* what concerns us because it helped us to adapt and evolve.

It's all about how we file our responses to habitat. According to studies done with infants and chimpanzees, we seem to exhibit a preference for regular and symmetrical patterns. And the fact that we tend to transform incoming information into the structure of the information already stored in our brain results in a certain satisfaction in finding relations. In some odd Kantian sense, human beings are wired to discern form in whatever they encounter. And this "perceptual bias" must certainly figure into any theory of aesthetics.

Although it seems fairly evident that we favor regularity and repetition over disorder and unpredictability (the brain stores the former more easily, thereby making these properties relevant to survival), this doesn't really explain why some people find art or beauty more important than others do. Even assuming a correlation between our response to art and our ancestors' response to nature, psychologists and philosophers may disagree about the aesthetic experience itself. Steven Pinker, an experimental psychologist, acknowledges the existence of pleasure centers in the brain, but he treats art as "pure pleasure technology" that does little more than trigger these centers in order to deliver "little jolts of enjoyment." The pleasure that we feel is not only biologically pointless, it is merely pathological: no higher purpose is being served by it.

Joseph Carroll, however, takes issue with Pinker. Carroll, a literary critic, contends that in addition to the obvious primordial aspect of art, there is a more contemplative and analytic pleasure to be had when the mind is free to engage the work. Sensory stimulation can be enhanced by a sort of informed reverie that embraces the work in all its subtlety and complexity, thereby adding to the pleasure we feel — which naturally and predictably brings us back to the idea of disinterestedness. And so, in the end, we're stuck with that subjectivism that does not permit me to know whether I derive less or more pleasure from eating an ice cream cone or from reading a sonnet than you do.

By now it is clear that beauty is a minefield: any observation one makes about it usually blows up in one's face. But I have decided to offer a few thoughts anyway. "Beauty" seems suited to those experiences that stop us in our tracks.

Whether it's a painting called *Broadway Boogie-Woogie* or a scherzo by Paganini, the beautiful is conducive to stillness. It doesn't excite us, or necessarily instill in us the desire to replicate it; it simply makes us exist as though we're existing for that very experience. I don't think I am speaking for myself alone in framing a period of time – before the critical faculties kick in – when we know that there is something beyond the usual twaddle. We know there is beauty. There is organic beauty and ornamental or decorative beauty. There is the beauty of the moment and of the moment gone ("The blackbird whistling or just after"). There is the beauty of words, of song, of color, and of design. Hogarth identified a line of beauty, and that line was curved; and Leopold Bloom, sitting in a pub, found himself staring at an oak bar, musing, "Beauty: it curves, curves are beauty."

In one way or another, each of us is a connoisseur of beauty. Elegance, economy of movement; particular combinations of color, sound, and substance; a fusion of purpose, function, and action – all make an impression on us, though the impression may vary. To some, logic is beautiful; to others, a painting by Vermeer. You may prefer a *Gymnopédie* by Satie to Maria Callas singing *"Ebben? Ne andrò lontana"* from *La Wally*. I may not. It doesn't matter. Beauty is everywhere; it's just not always present. One can find it in the line of a dress, in a line of poetry, in the line of a shoulder; it may be in the face of a girl "when all the wild summer was in her gaze," and it is forever in the face of Charlie Chaplin at the end of *City Lights*. And yet when we try to account for moments like these, words seem a poor choice for language.

Perhaps this vulnerability to beauty, as well as our inability to explain it, stems from the fact that beauty is fleeting. It is fleeting when fixed on walls, pinioned to matting, recorded on digital grooves, or printed on the page. It is fleeting even when we're gazing at the stars or across Lake Como. None of us exists in a state of perpetual delight or wonder, and even the most exalted works of art and nature do not always affect us with the same intensity. Indeed, the paradoxical question arises: if beauty were not temporary, would it last? Beauty may, in fact, exist only because it disappears, because it offers a glimpse of redemption in a world where such redemption is just an idea. That's why we spend so much time talking about it. (If we existed in a state of grace, talking about grace would be irrelevant.)

We talk about beauty because it matters – because whenever we stumble across it or remember how a poem or piece of music makes us feel, we think that beauty can save us. Beauty *should* save us, damn it. Doesn't each of us feel that "if everyone else felt about beauty the way I do," there'd be peace in the world?* Because that's what beauty does: it instills a sense of peace; it rids us of doubts and misgivings; it is, for as long as it exists, *all* that exists. And it gives us hope. It gives us hope until we recall, or have George Steiner recall for us, the Nazi camp kommandant who sent thousands of human beings to the gas chamber daily, and in the evening retired to his room, placed a record on the gramophone, and found himself transported by the opening chords of a Bach cantata. It's hard to believe that beauty will not make us kind. But, then, what poem ever stopped a war, what rose ever put a lion off his leap?

The problem with language – to tweak a lyric of Noel Coward's – is that too often the wrong people use it. Those who programmatically explain beauty or demonstrate where

---

* In Kant's system, a conditional "aesthetic imperative" characterizes our response to natural beauty – that is, we assume that others, in the presence of such beauty, must respond as we do.

it has gone wrong never manage to get it right. Beauty is elusive; it has to be. The reason, of course, lies with consciousness itself, with that old bugbear "dualism" that never hibernates for very long and that, sooner or later, undermines the quest for absolute knowledge. Nonetheless, one can believe in meaning without necessarily believing that life has any. I don't offer this as a paradox but as the limitation of a mind that hasn't accepted the possibility of a soul. To such a mind, which resists systematic conceptions of the cosmos, a chance phrase may sometimes encapsulate a view of the world that seems, if not absolutely right, then the best that we can do: "*Man is hungry for beauty. There is a void.*" The verdict is Oscar Wilde's, and it's one we might easily set aside. It is not witty. It is not novel. It's not even informative. Actually, it's rather simplistic. What does it tell us that we don't already know? "Man is hungry for beauty. There is a void." Nine words. Take a moment. Say them aloud. What else is there to be said?

My Holocaust
Problem

I DID NOT READ Daniel Goldhagen's *Hitler's Willing Executioners*. Nor have I read Raul Hilberg's *The Destruction of the European Jews*, or David Wyman's *The Abandonment of the Jews*, or, for that matter, any of the hundreds of well-received books about the fate of European Jewry between 1941 and 1945. With the exception of Primo Levi's *The Drowned and the Saved*, none of the survivors' accounts of the German atrocities have found their way into my hands. Incredibly, I have never so much as glanced at *The Diary of Anne Frank*, and except for inadvertently viewing a few minutes of Claude Landsmann's *Shoah*, I've also managed to avoid just about all of the documentaries that touch on the subject. I have, of course, been confronted by photographs of rounded-up Jews and footage of the camps when they were "liberated," a word that seems bitterly inappropriate when applied to the *lagers*. And finally, I regret to say, I saw *Schindler's List*, a film that despite its good intentions and air of somber rectitude seemed so slick and manipulative

73

that it transformed meaningless death into a story for sentimentalists and children.

My reluctance to examine the historical evidence does not stem from any reasoned position and should not be taken as a reflection on those – Jews and non-Jews alike – who immerse themselves in these materials. If such reluctance has any significance, it is that my family, like countless others, fell under the heel of the German boot: All four of my grandparents were either murdered or died in a concentration camp; my father was interned in a Russian labor camp, and his youngest sister was one of a handful of fighters who survived the Warsaw Ghetto Uprising in April 1943. So you might say I am either entitled, or not entitled at all, to keep my distance from such knowledge.

Nor is my aversion typical or atypical of the children of survivors. I know a dozen such children, themselves now middle-aged men and women, some who want to learn as much as possible about what happened to their parents and grandparents, while others prefer to avert their eyes. As for survivors themselves, most in my experience no longer try to repress their memories. On the contrary, they regard those memories as an obligation to speak out. They also watch the films, read the books, and attend the memorials honoring the Jewish dead. There is nothing strange, perhaps, in the fact that survivors tend to be less squeamish than their children when revisiting the words and images that both consecrate and desecrate their lives. It is, after all, who they are. To them, America, despite having been their residence for more than half a century, has never really become *home*; it has remained on some level an alien, if hospitable (and sometimes unintelligible) country that has never truly taken the place of the *platzes* and boulevards, the shtetls and ghettos of the world they knew as children.

That world is gone: the world of youth movements;

children's sanatoriums; and meetings of the Bund or the *Hashomer Hatzair*, with their impassioned debate over the pros and cons of socialism, communism, and Zionism. As for us, their offspring, born or raised in America, the cities and villages of Eastern Europe – Lodz, Wilna, and Kraców – are place-names only. We may learn about the plays our parents saw, or the books they read, or the songs they sang, but it is doubtful that we will ever understand what has been lost. It's like wanting to taste the bread they ate, or hear the sounds of the *Hoyf* (courtyard) where they lived, or smell the odors of the shops where they bought their butter and fish. Had Hitler killed thirty thousand or even three hundred thousand Jews, that world would have endured. But it was precisely this possibility that Hitler meant to eliminate.

Although a number of Jews did manage to survive, their world did not. More than villages and neighborhoods disappeared, more than the intangible awareness of familiar experiences was forever denied the living; a language – and everything a language signifies – was altered. After the war, Yiddish could never again be an unself-conscious form of expression; it, too, was now out of time; it, too, was something that had survived. Although children and adults may still learn to speak and read Yiddish easily, it is a different language from that spoken by my parents' generation. For us, Yiddish is made up of words; it is not a way of thinking and being, although at the same time it is a language that summons up the poignancy of a life and a culture irretrievably lost. And make no mistake, such knowledge is a burden. Insignificant though this burden is compared to the one carried by my parents' generation, it has acquired an almost congenital identity, as if we'd been born with a wound received by our ancestors.

One could, it is true, ignore it and adopt a way of life that has nothing to do with what happened. There may be, there probably are, children of survivors for whom English poetry or baseball takes precedence over more recent history. Still, for those who do not turn from self-knowledge, a prosaic lesson awaits. We are all, in one way or another, victims of our parents, so the question becomes: how do I accommodate what they and others like them suffered? In other words, how do I remember?

This should not suggest that there is a shortage of reminders. There are Holocaust studies, Holocaust books, Holocaust movies, Holocaust museums, and even Holocaust walking tours. According to James Young's *The Texture of Memory*, "nearly every major American city is home to at least one, and often several, memorials commemorating aspects of the Holocaust." That seems hard to credit, though the word's ubiquity can hardly be denied. And I have a problem with the word, as I have a problem with any word or phrase whose meaning is eroded by endless repetition. The more sophisticated the society, the more shorthand synonyms it musters to express the inexpressible. Indeed, I suspect that a more primitive civilization validates the right of noncommunication and is naturally respectful of what cannot be spoken of. Instead of trying verbally to encapsulate a calamitous event, a North American Indian or Inuit might refer to it as "that which cannot be spoken of without sorrow and despair."

And then there is *that* number, the "six million." Said enough times, it becomes more a mantra than the actual fact of six million human lives snuffed out. Said enough times, it makes the millions of non-Jewish dead seem less significant. Furthermore, six million did not die. It was one hundred thousand more or two hundred thousand less than six million. Odd how simple it is to round off so many thousands of people. But we do it because even if we had a more accurate count, it would be too cumbersome to say "five million eight hundred and twenty six thousand, three hundred and four"; and, anyway, that figure would be only *less* unreliable and obviously far more difficult to remember.

How do we fathom it when numbers take the place of human beings? How do we move individually from six human beings to six million dead? One way to understand is to look around and regard the members of one's own family: parents, brothers, sisters, aunts, uncles, and cousins, each with his or her own face and facial expressions, mannerisms, distinctive laugh or sneeze, and odd or conventional ideas. Now multiply these dozen or so people by five hundred thousand. Does the loss sink in? Or imagine if each one of the six million were a tiny razor cut on your skin, how many such nicks would it take before you'd be a raw exposed mass of nerves and capillaries? Ten thousand nicks? If so, that's one six-hundredth or 0.167 percent of those who died.

If we cannot speak of it – though speak of it we must – how do we remember it? Which is tantamount to asking: How do we understand it? The murder of millions may have no more meaning than the stupid malevolence of human beings, but there is also a compulsion to transubstantiate the reality of being rounded up and slain, to justify the idea of wholesale acquiescence. It is said they went like sheep, and I, for one, see nothing shameful in being rounded up like a sheep when one has no forewarning, or, if forewarned, no belief in the prospect of butchery, or, if belief, no natural proclivity or the means to defend oneself. Why should these people of the shtetl believe they were important enough to be killed en masse? The enemy this time was not a bunch of drunken Cossacks bent on flogging, burning, or rampaging; from such vicious thugs one knew enough to hide or flee. But from the Germans? From the state? Why should the state demand the slaughter of a people? And

not being able to grasp it, many Jews, initially at least, and unthinkingly, aided their murderers.

It is not the Jewish response that is incomprehensible but the German enterprise. When imagining pogroms, which are the violent outbursts of an oppressed lower class looking for scapegoats, and which might be viewed almost as an eco-ethnological hazard, like living near a volcano (I say this without overlooking the moral culpability of Poles, Ukrainians, Latvians, and Lithuanians), we recoil but sense in such violence the nature of the beast. But what are we to make of the systematic extermination of an entire people by a military power whose greatest concern was for the well-being of its executioners (hence Zyklon-B and Jewish labor to spare the sensibilities of German soldiers)? Except for the fact that it happened, it doesn't even seem possible.

Part of its incomprehensibility, of course, derives from a cultural bias. That it happened in Western Europe in the modern era and was carried out by a civilized people is an abomination so troubling that it puts the lie to humanness itself. It throws the moral world into disarray. To think about it and not flinch, to imagine what it must have been like – if one is not predisposed to accept divine providence – is to sneer at the very idea of God. Therefore, we try to make the Final Solution into something else: a part of God's plan, a necessary step for the creation of Israel, and we confer upon the dead the mantle of martyrdom. But in truth it is a story with no meaning and very few martyrs (Arthur Ziegelbaum, who committed suicide in London to call attention to the gas chambers, and Adam Czerniakov, chairman of the Warsaw *Judenrat*, who preferred suicide to sending more Jews to the gas chamber, being two notable exceptions). These millions of human beings did not die for a cause; they died because they were there and because they were Jewish.

And there was, and there is, no sense to it. Such wholesale suffering without purpose is obscene, which is why Theodor Adorno's oft-quoted phrase about the moral implausibility of poetry after Auschwitz rings true. Yet it is a truth without practical relevance, since the living have no choice but to articulate what they learn from history. Art does not stop where morality ends, nor does it simply take up where morality falters. Art and Auschwitz may appear to exist in separate universes, but both, in fact, are part of human nature, despite each one's inability to shed light on the other. Novelists and filmmakers may try, but any attempt at an aesthetic rendering, so it seems to me, can only alter the experience. As Irving Howe pointedly observed, there is an "intolerable gap between the aesthetic conventions and the loathsome realities of the Holocaust." What seems more essential – indeed, what is incumbent upon us – is not to transfigure what happened. We should seek neither to make sense of it nor invest it with a higher purpose nor assign blame to anyone except the Germans and their helpers. The Holocaust, which required the cooperation of thousands and the conscious indifference of millions, simply reveals that the human heart still beats in the inhuman breast.

Perhaps I should acknowledge at this point that my own family has always been wary of the commemorative functions surrounding the Holocaust. Official displays of grief make them uncomfortable. Memory – to state what is not always obvious – is personal, and therefore public testimonials, no matter how well meaning, possess an air of inauthenticity; they smack of state-approved history, of a reality that citizens are *supposed* to believe. The fact that the events in question happened, and happened in the manner presented, does not dispel the sense that one is still being told what to remember and what to feel. "There's no business like Shoah business," children of survivors say with chilly humor. Indeed, the conspicuous proliferation of books, films, museums, photographs, and artifacts – not to mention the solemn and tremulous visits to the sites of the *lagers* and the exhibitions of shoes, gold fillings, dust from the ovens, and railroad cars – have assumed the trappings of a secular religion, whose sacred objects are an analogical counterpart to Christian iconography with its splinters from the cross and its shroud of Turin.

One must be careful where reverence is concerned. In "The Joys and Perils of Victimhood," a wonderfully discerning essay in the *New York Review of Books*, Ian Buruma cautioned not only that these mementos are in danger of becoming kitsch (an "expression of emotion which is displaced") but that the authenticity of memory itself is at risk when identity is so closely bound up with ancestral suffering. Buruma asks the right question: "What is going on when a cultural, ethnic, religious or national community bases its communal identity almost entirely on the sentimental solidarity of remembered victimhood?" For one thing, what is going on is that Jews, for reasons both emotional and political, have turned the Holocaust into a hallowed icon and, by so doing, have encouraged other minorities to look for their own holocausts, the better to shore up *their* communal identities. For Buruma and others, this is an unhealthy and ahistorical form of self-definition: when the calamitous event takes center stage, history itself is gradually subverted.

Much of this soul searching about the implications of Holocaust remembrance was occasioned by the publication in 1999 of Peter Novick's *The Holocaust in American Life*. Novick, let it be said immediately, dislikes the idea that no greater suffering than the Holocaust has ever been visited upon a people, and he disapproves of the aura of sanctimony that began to surround it in the early 1960s. In fact, the genocide needed time to become the Holocaust. At first, survivors spoke of it in whispers and only among themselves. When a memorial was suggested in New York City a few years after the war ended, prominent Jewish organizations demurred, claiming it would represent "a perpetual memorial to the weakness and defenselessness of the Jewish people." But after the Adolf Eichmann trial in 1961 and Israel's Six-Day War in 1967, the observance of the genocide gradually emerged as a civic duty. Secular and assimilated Jews were now able to embrace a legitimate Jewish identity by defining themselves through an awareness of great suffering. Analyzing Israeli secularism, Tom Segev observed in *The Seventh Million*: "Emotional and historical awareness of the Holocaust provides a much easier way back into the mainstream of Jewish history without necessarily imposing any real personal moral obligation [such as actual religious belief would entail]. . . . The 'heritage of the Holocaust' is thus largely a way for secular Israelis to express their connection to Jewish heritage."

If all this was simply a means to get closer to one's heritage, it would not be so bad. But such expressions of kinship have unfortunately become like a victimization sweepstakes: the more one beats one's breast, the more one can lay claim to being authentically Jewish. The point at which a feeling of victimization becomes trivial is hard to define, but we know it when we hear it. It occurred when Woody Allen invoked his knowledge of survivors' accounts to explain how he was able to cope with the scandal involving his relationship with his girlfriend's adopted daughter. It occurred when Clarence Thomas resorted to the word "lynching" in characterizing his treatment at the hands of the Senate Judiciary Committee. By wrapping themselves in dire historical precedent, Thomas and Allen succeeded only in trivializing the suffering of African Americans and European Jews.

Needless to say, it isn't the survivors themselves who need to bring up the Holocaust to feel Jewish, but their children and grandchildren, who, as if to compensate for not having been born earlier, now take pains to make sure that the *lagers* will never be forgotten. Unhappily, it is but a small step from compulsory remembrance to vigorous marketing – from such flagrant examples as press releases for "Never Forget" galas to the changing of Primo Levi's title from *Se questo è un uomo* (If This Is a Man) to *Survival in Auschwitz*. Not a large transgression, one might think, but isn't the English title really a deliberate and audacious deception intended to sell books? Moreover, the aura of piety and privilege that attaches to survivors does not necessarily sit well with survivors themselves – not because they wish to put the Holocaust behind them, but because it all begins to seem self-serving, and even exculpatory, as though it may forgive them their sins. There are plenty of survivors, for example, who look askance at fellow survivors who they believe are making hay out of the Holocaust. Apparently, the high fees, limos, and three-star hotels some of these spokesmen require when speaking about their experiences do not go down well. "*Es shmekt nisht* (It smells wrong)," the others say.

Memory in the service of a national or ethnic cause is a two-edged sword. People have a right to make sure that the evils suffered by their parents and grandparents are not forgotten, but might there not be, in fact, a loss rather than a gain in understanding when testimonials to the Holocaust are forced on the public? This constant exposure, these excessive demonstrations of suffering do not always have the desired effect. To non-Jews, it may appear that these memorials and mementos have become nothing more than a point of pride for Jews, a means of self-congratulation. And though the "we suffered, we were there" Whitmanesque incantation may strengthen the bond among Jews, it has the effect of making everyone else an outsider.

There is something else to consider: the presumption that these conferences and memorials demonstrate the persistence of memory in something more than a ceremonial sense. The occasional ritualistic display of grief is all well and good, but how many of those who participate later set aside a minute to mourn? I know that my own American-born Jewish friends spend little time or emotion reflecting on what was lost. I am not suggesting that they ought to do more or that the Holocaust should color their lives — far from it. To suffer more would be to give the Germans and their helpers an even greater victory. All I am saying — and I am sorry to say it — is that there is a fundamental difference between those who are close to what happened and those with no familial connection to it.

Jews, as Jews well know, spend an inordinate amount of time and print discussing who is and who is not authentically Jewish. Orthodox Jews look askance at reform Jews; secular Jews have no truck with the Hasidim. I myself used to think that Jews who could not converse in Yiddish weren't really Jewish, just a kind of watered-down version, no matter how often they went to shul. For the children of survivors, the question is irrelevant. If secular, we are not only Jews, we are, in a manner of speaking, second-generation Jews, as if the German atrocity was so extraordinary that it put a stop to ordinary time and began a new consciousness of reality. Our birthright is a combination of shame, grief, and anger — with anger, I hope, being the dominant emotion. Why do I say this? Because one has a right to resent not only the death of people but also the birth of the memories that were forged in the camps, because what was lost in the camps besides so many lives was the potential for an uncomplicated happiness in the survivors and, to a lesser extent, in their children.

But how do we express this sense of loss without implying that we, as a people, are more deserving of the world's attention (and sympathy) than others who have experienced great suffering? Asking such a question does not mitigate the horror, nor does it diminish the special nature of the barbarous German undertaking. There *was* something special about the Holocaust, not in the numbers of dead but in the very determination to achieve those numbers. An entire race of people had been condemned to death by a klatch of German bureaucrats. This brooks no dispute. Yet somehow the literal and terrible truth of so much death must be rendered without plaintiveness, without kitsch, and without that sense of privilege that suffering seems to bring forth. In this respect, the interviews with survivors conducted by the YIVO Institute for Jewish Research, and Steven Spielberg's own archival project of establishing a permanent record of survivors' accounts, are worthy endeavors. Emotionally, however, this essentially private record of grief and memory is not sufficient for those who wish to remember in a more public way. How, then, shall we remember communally? More to the point, how do we ensure that memory does not become overly virtuous?

One thing we might do is remember not only how the living died but how they lived. To take the full measure of what the Germans did, we must learn about what was lost: the ordinary and the humdrum, the pleasures and peculiarities of home and work, all the taken-for-granted routines that once made up life in a city, village, or shtetl. We ought to familiarize ourselves with the modulated voices, the accords and discords, the diversity of opinion disseminated in letters, diaries, books, and plays (by 1939 there were around twenty Yiddish newspapers in Poland alone). Not one kind of Jew was destroyed, not one voice, or one accent, or one perspective, but a rich and vibrant culture and everything that culture contained and might one day have contained. There is a tendency, I think, when the numbers of the dead are so great, to feel that a monolithic entity has somehow fallen over the edge of the earth. The Jews of Europe were not just the short, dark-haired people we see in sepia-toned photographs wearing long coats and funny caps or babushkas. They *were* that, of course, but they were also much more; to believe anything else is a grave inaccuracy.

My aunt, who rarely spoke of the Warsaw Ghetto Uprising, had hoped that we would remember something else as well. In the few pages that she wrote about the uprising, she called attention to the people who had lived under the German occupation, conducting "a stubborn and harsh battle to stay alive in the Ghetto, a struggle to preserve their humanity." She thought we were already overlooking those who had foraged for food to feed the children, who set up makeshift hospitals and schools, who actually managed to put on plays and concerts – until the first *Aktions* and deportations began.

There is a flat stone in New York City's Riverside Park, near Eighty-third Street, embedded in pavement and encircled by iron grating. Not particularly imposing, the site draws little attention, and most people pass by without stopping. But afternoons of April 19, the anniversary of the Warsaw Ghetto Uprising, the stone, or *der shteyn* as it is known, hosts a gathering of survivors and their children. Seventy, perhaps eighty people attend, a fair number of them in their eighties and nineties. There are five or six speeches, some in English, some in Yiddish; afterwards, white roses are handed out and strewn over the rock. At the end, those who know

the words sing "The Partisan Hymn", and then everyone goes home. It's an unobtrusive ceremony in an out-of-the-way spot – and yet it seems more authentic than the grand and crowded demonstrations that take place in halls and
synagogues, attended by dignitaries and politicians. At *der shteyn*, people do not come to visit the past, they come because they remain part of the past.

Yet even here something is amiss. Engraved on the stone are these words:

THIS IS THE SITE FOR THE AMERICAN MEMORIAL TO THE HEROES OF THE WARSAW GHETTO BATTLE APRIL–MAY 1943 AND TO THE SIX MILLION JEWS OF EUROPE MARTYRED IN THE CAUSE OF HUMAN LIBERTY.

Not a sentiment one wants to dispute, and yet – and yet the words are not strictly true. To be a martyr, one has to sacrifice oneself for a cause, and the Ghetto fighters did not fight because they believed in liberty; they simply chose how they would die. As for the others, the vast number of others, death came because they had no means of escaping it. More human lives than one can imagine were first damaged, then expunged. An entire way of life was destroyed. Why say more than that?

I am not proposing a valediction forbidding representation. I am suggesting only that memory need not be virtuous and that the proliferation of Holocaust paraphernalia does not necessarily remind us of what has been lost. While scholarly books and serious documentaries about the Holocaust are invaluable in learning about what happened and why, a certain kind of excess breeds indifference, and even this essay may be in some measure a form of betrayal. There is a part of me that feels that whatever I say for public consumption somehow cheapens the suffering of those who died and those who survived. If I have any justification for writing this, it is that I promised my father I would present his alternative to the pomp and circumstance of remembrance. My father's idea is that Jews have a standard text, something short and simple, an agreed-upon narrative developed over time, like the *Megillah* recited during Purim, which would be read aloud on April 19, when families and friends gather privately to remember. They would gather not to honor the dead or resolve that it must never happen again, but simply to remember who it was that died and what it was that died with them.

POSTSCRIPT: In the end, no matter what writers write about, they write as writers, not participants. The discipline required to shape and arrange sentences keeps the brutal and messy facts at bay. This was made clear to me about a month or so after I began working on this piece. Quite by chance, I happened to catch on television the end of a documentary about the war against the Jews. There was graphic footage of Jews being shot in a ditch, of people arriving in Auschwitz, and of bodies being burned on the ground when there were simply too many for the crematoria to dispose of. The faces of the children were uncannily like the faces of children I played with when I was a child. I wanted to turn away, but I didn't. Although I would never have made a point of seeing this documentary, now that I was watching, it seemed both wrong and cowardly to turn away. In truth, it seemed imperative that I *not* turn away. I owed it to the murdered to watch. They suffered, and so should I, if only as a witness.

The question of degree – how much, to what extent, and how often do we remember? – may never have an adequate answer. After all, it is within parents' rights to protect their children not only from the gruesome footage but from the knowledge of what it represents, since such knowledge makes the uncomplicated idea of God and meaning difficult to comprehend. If the life of the mind is a series of steps involving the progressive loss of innocence, beginning with the realization that one is not the center of the universe and ending with the thought that the universe itself has no center, surely there is no need to accelerate a child's journey toward the programmed horror that the German leaders conceived for the Jews. People will come to such knowledge on their own, or they won't. I am not sure that the examined life requires the contemplation of what happened to the Jews. All I am sure of is that because those who perished had no choice in their deaths, we, their descendants, have no choice but to remember.

The Inexhaustible
Paul Valéry

T HE LIBERAL ARTS campus of l'Université Montpellier
in the south of France is named after the poet Paul Valéry
(1871–1945), which may come as a surprise, even to much
of the French populace. Valéry, after all, was not France's
greatest poet or her most influential man of letters, yet the
ministerial benediction seems apt. One cannot imagine, for
instance, l'Université Victor Hugo, or l'Université Sainte-
Beuve, or, saints preserve us, l'Université Charles Baudelaire.
The French, who have been known to bestow honors on both
tummlers and tumblers, in this case got it right. Valéry was
poet as pure thinker: a thinker who infused poetry with
sophisticated synoptic and musical techniques and a writer
who brought an almost desperate analytical fervor to his
own observations. He was also, famously, the poet who
abandoned verse for nearly two decades in order to devote
himself to more scientific, less sentimental pursuits.

Ambroise Paul Toussaint Jules Valéry was born in the
coastal town of Sète to a Corsican father and an Italian
mother, and spent his childhood in a house on a quay over-

looking the Mediterranean. When he was thirteen, the family (he had an older brother) moved inland to Montpellier, where Valéry attended the *lycée* and later studied law at the university. Never exactly a dedicated student, he was, however, a great reader, whose intellect was permanently ignited when a friend introduced him to mathematics and the music of Wagner. By then he had come across Viollet-le-Duc's prodigious *Dictionnnaire de l'architecture*, which also became something of an obsession; and when a copy of Baudelaire's translation of Edgar Allan Poe's work fell into his hands in 1889, he seemed far more impressed by Poe's "Philosophy of Composition" than by the poems themselves.

Still in his teens, Valéry exultantly published his first poem and embarked on life-long friendships with Pierre Louÿs and André Gide; it was Louÿs who introduced him to the person who would have the greatest influence on him, the Symbolist poet Stéphane Mallarmé. He also fell in love with an older woman, a certain Mme de Rovira, and suffered in silence until a chance encounter with her sent him spinning – sent him, in fact, toward the "crisis" that would set the tone for the next twenty-odd years. We're not exactly sure what precipitated this crisis. Nor does Valéry ever enlighten us. In a letter to Louÿs, he writes only that while visiting Paris he fell "victim to a coincidence which was the strongest of all those that had reduced me to absurdity during the years 1891 and 1892, and finally drove me to flight."

The presumably awkward event, coupled with his own doubts about the direction his life was taking, forced him to take stock of everything he believed. On the night of October 4, 1892, with a storm raging outside his room, Valéry stayed awake till dawn undergoing his own dark night of the soul. At the advanced age of twenty, he was experiencing what in the Existential fifties was called an "identity crisis," and it led him to the realization that he was too vulnerable to his own sensibility and even to literature itself, which he already regarded as "the art of playing with the souls of others." Skeptical of writers' tricks and words' easy effects, he wanted no part of them. Unwilling to write about his own feelings, he was at a loss to understand how other writers could shamelessly record theirs. As for verse, it, too, was literature; and literature, as he would one day note, "comprises a sort of politics and competitiveness, numerous idols, a devilish combination of priest and tradesman, of intimacy and publicity, indeed, of everything needed to frustrate its first-born aims."

Repudiating mental and emotional waffling, he elected to make himself over into someone immune to excessive feeling and anything that might obfuscate thought. He imposed on himself "a sort of severity – a rigorous discipline to save [himself] from the jaws of stupidity." How would he go about this? In a letter of 1898 he writes, entirely without irony:

> *Au fond c'est bien simple* – you reduce everything to sensations and mental phenomena, you regroup these into two or three classes according to their properties of substitution, you look for a comprehensive relationship between all these factors of cognition, etc.; and you have in your hands a means of analysis entirely general and new. . . . According to the use you want to make of it you adopt one of these ways, literature, philosophy, criticism or imagination etc. etc.

In short, he decided that verbal formulas based on a mathematical model were alone capable of expressing his thoughts with absolute clarity. It's not that he wanted to remove passion from the equation; it's just that he believed more passionately in the equation than in its parts. And

ARTHUR KRYSTAL

this attempt to understand *how* he thought would, he surmised, affect *what* he thought. To this end he gave up literature and the writing of poetry and became his "own and only confidant."

92

Valéry was not the first writer to put literature behind him. Nearly three centuries earlier the author of the *Discours de la méthode* announced that he had "entirely given up the study of letters, resolving to seek for no other science than that which [he] could find within himself, or at least in the great book of nature." Descartes made good on his promise, but it can't be said that he spent most of his life investigating his own psyche. Valéry did, or, at any rate, did his best. So began what some have called Valéry's "long silence," which turns out to be something of an exaggeration. Unlike Alfred de Vigny and Rimbaud before him, or J. D. Salinger in our own time, the only thing Valéry stopped writing was poetry. He continued to write letters and reviews; he finished an intoxicating Socratic dialogue, *Introduction à la méthode de Léonard de Vinci*, as well as the wry and spooky *La Soirée avec Monsieur Teste*. He also, in 1894, began keeping a daily journal of his thoughts, which over the next fifty years would expand into some twenty-six thousand pages. Hardly what one would call a silence. Nor, for that matter, did he retreat into a monastery or even into himself.

A year or so after his "crisis" he moved to Paris, where he rented a small room in the rue Gay-Lussac. He put up a sign: "*Méfie-toi sans cesse!*" (Be always on your guard!) and set up a blackboard on which he solved various mathematical problems. He put away Balzac and Hugo and picked up the works of Newton, Laplace, Kelvin, Faraday, Maxwell, Riemann, and Poincaré. Although he arose each morning at 5 A.M. and scribbled in his *Cahiers de Notes* until 8 A.M.

(the hours "between the lamp and the sun"), he was by no means a recluse. He saw Gide and Louÿs, his friendship with Mallarmé deepened, and on Tuesday evenings he attended the literary gatherings at the poet's home. Tuesday nights with Mallarmé were by then a Parisian institution, and the names of those who dropped by included Verlaine, Manet, Degas, Huysmans, Heredia, Gauguin, Gide, Claudel, Laforgue, Wilde, Yeats, Bernard Shaw, Gabriele D'Annunzio, and Stephan George. All made their way to Mallarmé's house to hear its owner quietly hold forth on the meliorative powers of verse.

To make ends meet, Valéry took a secretarial position at the Ministry of War and later became the private secretary to an official of the Agence Havas. In 1900 he married Jeannie Gobillard, a niece of the Impressionist painter Berthe Morisot, who had been a good friend of the Mallarmés. They moved to a house on the rue de Villejust (now rue Paul Valéry). Eventually three children were born, and Valéry, to all appearances, was a middle-class fellow who went to work each day and returned home at night. Although he faithfully bent over his *Cahiers* each morning, by 1898 he had entirely stopped writing for publication. And for the next fifteen years this man who had once lived for poetry did not attempt a single line of verse.

To stop writing poetry is not in the great scheme of things an earth-shattering event. Valéry's decision was certainly less incandescent than Rimbaud's guillotining of his muse at nineteen and subsequent departure for Africa. Rimbaud was a restless and imperious man-child whose abdication might be likened to kicking a habit or putting aside a tumultuous adolescence. (The usual analogy is to a fiery comet that quickly burns itself out.) Valéry, however, was more like a slowly revolving planet that corrected its own trajectory by casting off poetry. Whereas one feels, perhaps mistakenly, that Rimbaud threw away his life along with his art, one thinks that Valéry might have actually enriched his life, at least for a time, by subtracting poetry.

Still, one has to wonder why. The man was, after all, a poet, and you'd think that the early literary success, to say nothing of Mallarmé's encouragement, would have urged him on. But given his temperament, the same forces that drew him to poetry – that is, a sensibility that demanded absolute precision and perfection from the literary work – also repelled him. He could not abide vagueness, sentimentality, or technical shoddiness. And the French language is a tough *petit four*. Poetry in English is, of course, a matter of stresses between consonants. "Take care of the consonants," Bishop Whately advised, "and the vowels will take care of themselves." With French, the situation is reversed. There are not six but nineteen vowels in French, and they are, as Valéry pointed out, *"très nuancées."* The poet therefore requires a precision instrument to construct the delicate verbal temples whose music is commensurate with their meaning. Like other poets who had become enamored of Wagner's operas, Valéry believed that all the arts should aspire to music. But an ideal is precisely that which cannot be made concrete: "What written page," Valéry asked, "can attain the heights of the few notes of the Grail motif?"

Valéry came of age when one could without self-consciousness speak of beauty and the absolute. It was the reason one made art and the reason one was doomed to fail. "Nothing so pure can exist with the circumstances of life," Valéry wrote. "We only traverse the idea of perfection as a hand passes with impunity through a flame; but the flame is uninhabitable." Those who ostentatiously staked a claim to art only annoyed him. Valéry distrusted inspiration, disliked enthusiasm, loathed false profundity, and wasn't very fond of the real thing either. Although he was familiar with the Parnassian school as well as the more confessional poets who worked in *vers libéré* (soon to become *libre*), Valéry's appreciation was tempered by the rift between the sublime and the poor notations on the page that sought to attain it. Even the Symbolist poets, who had the right idea about revealing a hidden reality through indirection and imagery, could not often meet his exacting standards. Moreover, there already existed a poet whose work seemed to embody everything Valéry demanded of the art. Mallarmé's poetry was original, allusive, elliptical, and musically evocative. Mallarmé used language, Valéry noted, as if he had invented it. If Mallarmé was perfection on the page, how could Valéry improve on it?

Anxiety of influence, however, does not altogether explain Valéry's self-imposed silence. His preoccupation with music, architecture, and mathematics persisted through the years, and he was drawn to them precisely because their "language" was unmediated: no words were required. In truth, he distrusted words and thought them incapable of lucidly expressing his ideas. "If I were to attempt to produce a philosophy for myself (may God forbid)," he observed, "I should begin by completely rewriting my dictionary." Clarity! Rigor! Precision! Nothing less would do. And though his affection and admiration for Mallarmé never waned, Valéry was after something else: "For him the work; for me, the Self." Just as some people go to the gym to build up their biceps and lats, Valéry spent three hours every morning mapping, shaping, and elaborating his thoughts. All writers are self-conscious, but Valéry was an interior cosmologist of the first order, honing self-awareness to a point where every thought was, additionally, a thought about itself. And this, of course, is just as infinitely regressive as it sounds.

But Valéry was not intimidated. Scientific thinking would organize cognizance into distinct components, and everything – from describing a stone to constructing a church – would become a question of identification, separation, and elimination. Indefiniteness repelled him. Who else but Valéry could pray: "Deliver us from the immiscible."

And because the Multiplicity helps those who help themselves, Valéry followed developments in relativity, quantum theory, wave mechanics, group and set theory, topology, differential equations, and thermodynamics. This was no physics-for-poets curriculum; the man was in earnest and applied what he learned. We can find traces of Valéry in Heidegger, Wittgenstein, Merleau-Ponty, Paul Ricoeur, Sartre, Barthes, and Derrida. In fact, it's safe to say that of every poet who ever wrote in any language (and this includes Goethe), Valéry was probably the most scientific and philosophic minded – not in the poems so much as in the *Notebooks* that slowly and surely led him back to poetry.

The best way to characterize the *Notebooks* is to reproduce them – all twenty-six thousand pages; otherwise, they sound like something out of a story by Borges. Here is a mind determined to reject all idols, accept its own ignorance, cleanse language of unnecessary vocabulary, and enter into its own workings, becoming, as it were, part of the machinery. Thinking, for Valéry, was *active*: a vital force generated by specific principles, which ordered the flow of perceptions before thoughts could occur. In this, Valéry was strictly a Kantian, arguing intuitively that before we can have information things must be *in formation*. "Our philosophy is determined by its apparatus, not by its object," he wrote. "It cannot be separated from its difficulties, which constitute its *form*." And if he could (by watching himself think) discover the model that mental operations depended on, he could then build his thoughts in much the same way that an architect (by mastering principles of physics and engineering) builds beautiful and monumental structures. One might be permitted a doubtful sniff, but as Henri Bergson noted, "What Valéry has done, had to be attempted."

To get a sense of what he was up to, you may want to spend an evening with *Monsieur Teste*, the work written not long after Valéry began his daily abstractions. In *Teste* we first encounter the phrase that would, in one form or another, reappear in the *Notebooks* and the later poems: "I am being and seeing myself; seeing myself see myself." Teste is Valéry distilled, the totally self-sufficient individual who claims: "I am at home in MYSELF. I speak my own language, I hate extraordinary things. Only weak minds need them. Believe me literally: genius is *easy*."*

The usual charges leveled against Valéry include solipsism, narcissism, and an absence of feeling. None of these aspersions seems right, or wholly right. Valéry was not taken with himself; he was simply interested in himself; and there is a world of difference between the two. The fact that he doesn't emote on the page neither dismisses nor refutes a passionate nature. The man had feelings; he just didn't want to have them, and he certainly wasn't going to go public with them. Nor, for that matter, does a mathematical mind or scientific temper preclude the poet's eye, or the painter's either. Valéry's sumptuous descriptions of Leonardo's work are astonishing in their tender regard. He both loved and admired the Florentine's ability to combine grand conceptual schemes with lush, intimate details.

---

* In *A Letter from Madame Émilie Teste*, we learn that her husband calls her by a number of names. Sometimes he calls her "Being"; sometimes, "Thing"; and sometimes "Oasis." "But," as she observes, "he never tells me that I am stupid – and this touches me profoundly." In other words, Valéry could smile.

Indeed, it's Leonardo's *Notebooks*, which Valéry consulted in the Bibliothèque Nationale in 1894, that inspired his own multitudinous journals with their musings and meditations, fragments, neologisms, drawings, and watercolors. Valéry, in fact, considered the *Notebooks* his "real" work, and in number of words they dwarf the poems, essays, and dialogues; they are, as the editors of the most recent edition aptly note, "the huge, submerged part of the iceberg of which the published work is only a fraction."

This is the fourth attempt to classify what is essentially unclassifiable, and the first to reproduce in English every line of the original 260 chapbooks in which Valéry wrote. Editing the *Cahiers* is a monumental undertaking, and Brian Stimpson, Paul Gifford, and Robert Pickering have acquitted themselves honorably. The first two volumes of the projected series give every indication of meticulous research and scholarship. The books are handsome; the typeface is delicate but readable; and the endnotes are what endnotes are supposed to be: enlightening addenda served up in pithy, eloquent prose. As for the variegated content, it will eventually be distributed throughout five volumes, each volume organized around similar, though not necessarily interrelated, themes. The first volume offers up: ego, activity, eros; the second: art, poetry, literature; the third: psychology, sensibility, memory, and so on. As the editors make plain, the *Notebooks* are more than just another of Valéry's works, something supplemental to the poems and criticism; they are in a sense responsible for everything he wrote after 1913.

Let other people make books, Paul Valéry would make his mind – an ambition so grand, so charged with psychological import, that literally hundreds, perhaps thousands of entries simply cannot measure up to his plan for them. And this, unfortunately, makes Valéry sometimes more interesting to read about than to read in. But for every intellectual wriggle that seems commonplace or just plain wrong ("Reading Flaubert is intolerable to a man who thinks") or that seems right but really isn't ("A poem is to a novel as sound is to a noise"), there are scores of statements that tickle the fancy ("I would rather have composed a mediocre work in all lucidity than a brilliant masterpiece in a state of trance"). Furthermore, you never have to read far before he sets your mind humming: "What is most beautiful is of necessity tyrannical." Is he right? Perhaps. But if he isn't, he forces you to figure out why. As the fragments mount up, one is reminded here and there of Voltaire, of Kant, of Nietzsche, of Wilde, and dozens of others. The man was relentless. "Your duty is to exhaust," he told himself. And he did: he feasted on himself; he binged on ideas; and the reader should be prepared to do the same.

But let's be clear: Valéry never retired from the world. He read the newspapers, kept up a lively correspondence, met with friends, swam in the ocean, and told his children stories. And at age forty-eight, this supposedly cold fish took a mistress, one who caused him much joy and, yes, heartache too. Naturally, he would parse the act of sexual intercourse into its excitable components, characterizing it as a "machine emitting sighs ... An oscillation around a point of equilibrium." (The man couldn't help himself.) Nevertheless, the love affair shook him up, and the *Notebooks* reverberate from its shocks and aftershocks. If he lived only to analyze, he still had to live; it was a dualism without irony: feeling isn't banished to make room for the intellect; it's simply one more subject for the intellect to examine. Which is as good a way as any of describing Paul Valéry's return to poetry.

In 1912 the publisher Gaston Gallimard sent Gide to obtain Valéry's permission to reprint his early verse. Valéry declined. Not to be put off, Gallimard took already published poems, installed them in a new edition, and mailed it to the reluctant author. Valéry looked, read, tampered, and soon found himself drawn again to the act of composition. But being Valéry, he couldn't just sit down and write; he had to identify and delineate the elements that went into the poem's creation. Words alone were still not sufficient; the matter remained of small importance; and content was for weaklings. What Monsieur Valéry intended by a poem was something else:

> The most powerful "creations," the most splendid monuments of thought, have been derived from the considered use of voluntary *resistance* to our immediate and continuous "creation" of observations, narratives, and impulses. . . . Well-defined poetic rules . . . [are not] formulas of restricted creation. . . . Their fundamental aim is to lead to the complete and organized man. . . . These restrictions may be entirely arbitrary: it is enough that they hamper the natural and inconsequent flow of digression or gradual creation.

Although this may be viewed as an elaborate way of saying that tennis is played with a net, that's still saying a lot; it's the net, after all, that defines the game and is ultimately responsible for the skills necessary to avoid it. The creative act becomes, in effect, a system of transmutation through applied laws, a sort of corollary to the laws that transform perception into knowledge. Where Kant had as his categories (quantity, quality, modality, relation), Valéry proposes resistance, separation, elimination, proportion.

If you have ever wondered how a poet could write, "*Un poème est une sorte de machine à produire l'état poétique au moyen des mots*," now you know. Yes, the idea of the poem as a machine for producing the poetic state through words sounds ridiculously academic, but you have to understand how much value Valéry placed on machines. The human body is a machine, so is the brain, and no matter what our instincts shout, it's the mind that creates poetry, not the soul, not the heart. "In poetry I see nothing but conscious investigations, acceptance of exquisite 'shackles,' inflection of thought, and the perpetual triumph of sacrifice." Most writers and readers, I suspect, are loath to acknowledge the difference between fiction or poetry and pure thinking, though the difference is both natural and beneficial. Whatever makes a poem or novel great, it has nothing to do with a conceptual scheme whose power is generated by the power of reason. Valéry knew this and resented it. When a symposium of French writers was asked why each of them wrote, Valéry's answer was "out of weakness."

Naturally, music retained its preeminent position. Valéry wanted poetry to produce on the nervous system the same effects as music; and when he finally set to work on a new poem, one finger was plunking out a Gluck recitative on a piano. *La Jeune Parque* (The Young Fate), begun in 1913, was supposed to be his return and his farewell to poetry, but he was still at it four years later, when it was taken from him and published – to great acclaim. And while this didn't exactly light a fire under him, he continued to compose. In a letter to Louÿs, he described the poet as a combination of refined dreamer, judicious architect, wise algebraist, and infallible calculator of "the effect to be produced." The effect is created by a classical scheme employing involuted syntax, emblematic words, shifting phrase lengths (with each of those nineteen vowels playing off one another), and symbolic images whose sequence of associations is developed through harmonic modalities. In short, think early Stravinsky rather than Mendelssohn. The irony, of course, is too barbed to ignore: for a man so enamored of clarity, Valéry wrote some of the most obscure poems in the French language.

Although not the first poet who believed that thought in poetry is inseparable from the cadences that deliver it, Valéry may have been the first to state unequivocally that to arrive at a perfect fusion of form and content, you cannot begin with content. Not surprisingly, T. S. Eliot was a big fan. Not only did Eliot admire the poems, he thought Valéry's true worth lay in the fact that he had established a new image of the poet, someone who, in Valéry's words, "is no longer the disheveled madman who writes a whole poem in the course of one feverish night." But one may be permitted to dispute Valéry's own unpoetic self-portrait. Valéry may not have had the swagger of Byron or Baudelaire, but he felt the same desire to re-create himself through verse; this, too, is a form of passion. And for all the rigmarole about mathematical language, his own language could be both charming and tender (though this is lost in translation).

> *Ta forme au ventre pur qu'un bras fluide drape,*
> *Veille; ta forme veille, et mes yeux sont ouvert*

> Your form with pure belly that a flowing arm
> Guards, your form guards, and my eyes are open

In returning to poetry, Valéry did not detour around the *Notebooks*. He's still the archeologist of the mind; he's still digging. The epigraph to his most famous poem, "*La Cimetière marin*" (The Cemetery by the Sea) is from Pindar: "Do not, my soul, seek immortal life, but exhaust the field of the possible." The one thing poetry did alter in dramatic fashion was his social life. Slow to publish, Valéry was quick to garner fame. He became a public figure whose time was increasingly spent on essays, articles, lectures, and radio addresses. He traveled everywhere and met everyone – Conrad, Stravinsky, Rilke, Ortega y Gasset, and Einstein. In London he stood before an audience that included Virginia Woolf, Lytton Strachey, Aldous Huxley, Edmund Gosse, and Arnold Bennett. Honors and prizes befell him. He joined the Committee for Arts and Letters of the League of Nations; he was elected to the Académie Française; awarded an honorary doctorate from Oxford; made director of the Centre Universitaire Méditerranéen de Nice and president of the Société des Peintres-Graveurs Français, and given the Chair of Poetics at the Collège de France.

But the world that this public Valéry returned to was not the world that the private Valéry had begun to record in 1894. World War I had taken its toll. The appalling human losses, the waste and devastation, the gouged-out countryside brought him to the mournful conclusion that the mind itself had been cruelly injured. "Something deeper has been worn away than the renewable parts of the machine," he wrote. "Our fears are infinitely more precise than our hopes." Where once material progress had presumed mental progress, it now seemed that civilization, instead of saving us, was only finding more efficient means of destroying us. Suddenly, there appeared little reason to believe that man as a species would continue to grow wiser and more productive. "The future is not what it used to be," Valéry remarked. What seems now a cliché was at the time a startling reversal of thinking. "We are aware that a civilization has the same fragility as a life," Valéry wrote in

1919. "The circumstances that could send the works of Keats and Baudelaire to join the works of Menander are no longer inconceivable; they are in the newspapers."

In his general pessimistic outlook, Valéry is sometimes compared to that other conservative man of letters who lived across the channel. Both men had a background in philosophy, but one was a metaphysician while the other disapproved of all metaphysics. Valéry was tethered to the earth in a way that Eliot resisted; and his assessment of the human condition, however melancholy, possesses a sympathy lacking in Eliot's canon. Sometimes Valéry is given to overstatement: "Convictions are simply and secretly murderous." But then any extreme political position was bound to meet with his displeasure, since it suggested a mind closed to its own potential. About the Left, he had this to say: "The heart of the weak is hideous; anyone who suffers for a just cause or a creed has a poisonous serpent in his heart." About the Right, he identified its fatal flaw and eerily predicted a change in strategy, at least where a certain kind of compassionate conservative is concerned: "The rightists have never had brains enough to pretend they have a heart." And his disgust with what European culture had brought down upon itself led to a terrible summation: "Simply remember that between men there are two relations only: logic or war." In that one statement, he tells us everything we need to know about our chances of survival.

If most politicians met with Valéry's disdain, intellectuals fared no better. He referred to them as a tribe of *uniques* (prefiguring Harold Rosenberg's "herd of independent minds" by half a century) and likened them to demons frequently looking into paper mirrors. His own mirror reflected everything; a respect for law, tradition, and service (in his youth he had been an anti-Dreyfussard). He was, in fact, a nationalist, but one who could write, "We must have done with the fatal dogma of national sovereignty." Was he an elitist? Of course. He recognized the differences between men and knew what men were capable of. He understood that the relationship between the individual and the state is a far more subtle matter than which one takes precedence. His own striking example of the intensely private individual functioning in the public realm illustrates a simple truth: The individual cannot be more important than the state if the state is to survive, but if the state is to survive *honorably*, then the *idea* of the individual must be more important than the *idea* of the state.

Read enough of Valéry and you will stumble across contradictions, paradoxes, and qualifications. But that is to be expected. Sooner or later, a man like Valéry, if he lives long enough, is going to think of everything. He isn't so much inconstant as he is continuous; so nothing should surprise us – not even this:

> It seems to me that the soul alone with itself, and speaking to itself from time to time, between two *absolute* silences, never employs more than *a small number of words* and none that is *extraordinary*. That is how we know *there is a soul* at that moment.

The *Notebooks*, however, are a lexiconic whirlwind: notions, ideas, impressions, and nascent treatises are all swept along, pulled by the mind's rush to examine and file. The fragments astonish, seduce, illuminate, repel, bore, and agitate. There is danger here: to read Valéry seriously is to begin to question one's own seriousness. Why, for example, don't I regard the mind as an instrument that requires constant attention? Is it possible that I'm just an amalgam of ossified beliefs and convenient assumptions? Why am I not more skeptical about the things I take for granted? Why do I go to the movies when I can stay home and think or, at least, listen to Bach? Valéry took self-improvement to another level: yet try as he might, he never reached that intellectual Eden where truth and knowing fold together. He may have begun writing with the purpose of becoming "an 'I' for whom the tormented 'I' would be an object," but in the end the tormented "I" is still hanging around, still scowling into the pure gaze of the other "I."

Years after jotting down that there is "nothing more idiotic than the heart – in which Pascal thinks we should believe," Valéry surrenders: "My heart. It triumphs. Stronger than everything . . . this damn, sacred – H –." Has the old boy finally come round to thinking, along with his more emotional Irish contemporary, "O heart, O troubled heart"? Not quite, or at least not without getting in one parting, necessarily analytical, shot: " 'Heart' – is the wrong name for it. I would like – at least – to find the true name of this terrible resonator . . . all powerful – irrational – inexplicable, because not explaining itself." Valéry never did lie down in the foul rag and bone shop, but he knew where it was. He accepted finally that the heart has reasons that reason does not know, but that didn't mean that he couldn't try to parse and classify them. Perhaps no one ever tried harder.

Club Work

W. H. Auden, Lionel Trilling
& Jacques Barzun

*Poets and Professors and all those whose love of
books exceeds their love of automobiles will welcome a chance to save in excess of 50% on their
book purchases.* — W. H. Auden

THE LOVER OF books is a disgruntled beast. If it's not
Horace shaking a fist at multiplying poets in ancient Rome,
it's Dr. Johnson groaning under the weight of superfluous
authors in eighteenth-century London; if it's not Goethe de-
nouncing book reviewers in nineteenth-century Weimar, it's
Randall Jarrell lacing into supercilious critics in twentieth-
century New York. For every season there is a time under
heaven for complaining: "[I]n the degree that we have come
to take literature with an unprecedented, a religious, seriousness, we seem to have lost our pleasure in reading. More
and more young people undertake the professional study
of literature; fewer like to read." What seems like an apt
description of the state of literature studies circa 2000

appeared in a 1952 review of Edmund Wilson's *The Shores of Light*, and the reviewer, Lionel Trilling, seemed put out that reading, "which used to be an appetite and a passion, is now thought to be rather *infra dig* in people of intelligence." There is something else out of place about these sentences: they appeared in the publication of a book club whose stated purpose was the dissemination of the very books that Trilling despaired of ever being savored.

In 1951, Trilling, Jacques Barzun, and W. H. Auden had been enlisted by Trilling's former student at Columbia, Gilman Kraft, to form the editorial board of a fledgling publishing venture to be named the Readers' Subscription Book Club. Their duties would entail choosing books and writing monthly columns for the club's bulletin, the *Griffin*. Why would someone who believed that readers were becoming insensible to the pleasures of literature undertake such work? For one thing, Trilling probably believed it less than he made out; for another, he knew that however small the audience for books, it needed looking after. His bolder, more prescient point concerns the relation between the professional study of literature and the love of reading.

Shortly after the founding editors departed from the book club in 1963 (by which time it had been reincorporated as the Mid-Century Book Society), the deconstructionist gale blew in from across the Atlantic, upsetting the historic balance between readers and texts, between literature and criticism — thereby recasting the book-club essays by Auden, Barzun, and Trilling as some of the last examples of literary criticism aimed at a general audience by members of the academy.* Indeed, the fact that two professors

---

* This is not to dismiss the fine critical essays published in literary reviews and journals of public opinion after 1960; I mean simply that, as

in the humanities and a poet famous for his learning once deigned to head such a club speaks volumes, as it were, about the difference in the literary culture then and now.

One such difference, more felt than acknowledged, has been the almost complete bifurcation of literary criticism into the academic and the journalistic styles. Until the 1960s, literary prose was roughly divisible, as Cyril Connolly suggested, into the Mandarin and the Vernacular. The former rejoiced in complex sentences that took their sweet time to get to the point (the point may well have been the eloquent unfurling of one dependent clause after another), while the latter depended on familiar speech patterns and the brisk rhythms of journalism. Unlike in sensibility and syntax, the two styles nonetheless reflected an unwavering belief in the transparency of the written word. This faith in language, however, would soon be tested by Continental philosophers and semioticians who concluded that the problematic nature of mind and language required a style of discourse emblematic of this difficulty. Instead of borrowing from – and contributing to – the language of literature, academic critics began to generate an alternative parlance that, for want of a better word, became known as the Theoretical.

An implicit tenet of this new style, which was characterized by tortured syntax and a profusion of technical terms, was that everything written in the old style was somehow innocent of its own deeper implications. This, in turn, had the unintended effect of placing an intellectual barricade in front of any new lettristic movement; and so the progression of Classic-Augustan-Romantic-Victorian-Modern came to a standstill with Postmodernism, which

---

a rule, academics who discussed literature either in a general sense, or in terms of specific works, often did so without the common reader in mind.

has little to do with literature and everything to do with rapidly changing theoretical models: structuralism, deconstruction, reader-response theory, new historicism, postcolonialism, culture studies, gender studies, queer studies.

Whatever else may be said of the theoretical style, it showcases by default the organic relationship that once existed between literature and criticism. Whereas the theory-locked essay is not meant to be taken for a category of literature, the lettristic is an extension of the literary experience – is, in fact, in the right hands, a species of literature. One has only to think of essays by Samuel Johnson, Hazlitt, De Quincey, Stevenson, Arnold, Ruskin, Orwell, and the Henry James of the Prefaces. The literary essay, or more accurately the essay about literature, may have reached its apex during the second quarter of the last century, with the prestige conferred on it by T. S. Eliot, whose own efforts were models (certain of his opinions notwithstanding) of clarity, discernment, learning, and persuasiveness. With Eliot, the critical essay not only fed on the work of poets but enhanced it, providing an exegetical frame to set off the poem's colors and shadings. And modern literature, because it was complex and disturbing, because it openly equated form with function, brought forth critics intent on measuring the tension between the cultural implications of rhetoric and the autonomy intrinsic to unique works. Twenty years after the publication of "The Waste Land," we had reached, as Randall Jarrell famously said, the "Age of Criticism" – an age that relied on literature's preeminence in order to emerge.

An age of criticism naturally serves up critics unhappy with the age, and Jarrell's designation was not meant as an honorific. Criticism, he pointed out, "which began by humbly and anomalously existing for the work of art, and was in part a mere by-product of philosophy and rhetoric, has by now become, for a good many people, almost what the work of art exists for: the animals come up to Adam and Eve and are named – the end crowns the work." Jarrell was being disingenuous; critics were never so humble, and he knew it. His anxiety preceded the age, and it was only after his death that his cautionary remarks bore fruit. In fact, it was the Age of Criticism precisely because most critics would not have bothered to state that literature was more important than how they spoke about it. "Books were our weather, our environment, our clothing," Anatole Broyard recalled about his days in Greenwich Village in the 1950s. "We didn't simply read books; we became them. We took them into ourselves and made them into our histories." The only thing that mattered was the life of the mind, and everything relevant to that life – God, sex, politics, society – had to pass through the centrifuge of literature.

All this is to say that the literary critic labors under a burden that critics of the other arts do not. Unlike those who write about music, painting, or architecture, the literary critic relies on the same instrument used by the poet and novelist. No one asks that the critic's prose be equal to the creative writer's, only that it display a passionate advocacy of – or considered opposition to – the poem or novel's own heightened language. Passion can be mute, inarticulate, or eloquent – it can even be polemical – but it cannot be jargon ridden or willfully obscure. Awkward, even clichéd prose is forgivable, but to come to literature with the theorist's pride in complexity and obscurantism is like encountering a slightly demented lover who lavishes all his time and effort on a letter rather than on the person the letter is intended for.

I s there a right way to write about books? Edwin Denby, the dance critic at midcentury for the *Herald Tribune*, perhaps came close when he stipulated: "It is not the critic's historic function to have the right opinions but to have interesting ones." "Interesting" is not a terribly interesting word; it is, however, a somewhat deceptive one. To tweak a phrase: serious is easy, interesting is hard. But in the absence of a universal template, how does one go about being interesting?

In a 1955 talk, "On Not Talking," Trilling pronounced that the "most discouraging element in American cultural life was a lack of innocence and ready human respect, a fear of being wrong, an aspiration to expertise." (Isn't this the genome of the postmodernist?) Trilling, who was perhaps our most sophisticated reader of novels, sensed that knowledge itself is subject to hesitancies and uncertainties, and that literature is ground too fine to be poured into any one theoretical vessel. What Trilling was getting at was cultural sophistication that did not preclude openness on the part of the critic. Let the critic stumble, reverse himself, and question his own motives – why not? Isn't a critic surprised by his own response to literature preferable to one who thinks he has all the answers? We may want a critic whose reading has been seasoned by experience and whose experience is better informed for having read seriously, but we also want that critic to invigorate us, to clear the mind of unruly shrubbery, to broaden our perspective, not by being right, but by getting close enough to make us think about what is right.

It was a hill, really, that Montaigne lived on and drew his name from: it is only the Essays that are mountainous.

The House of the Dead is not Dostoevsky's greatest work but it is, perhaps, his least irritating.

One of my college teachers said that the day comes to
all men when they no longer delight in reading novels.

Thus begin some of the reviews and essays that Auden,
Barzun, and Trilling contributed to the *Griffin* and the *Mid-*
Century. In the post-Derridean classroom, one might argue
that these particular writers, through no fault of their own,
read books with a certain inbred naiveté, insufficiently aware
of an author's cultural assumptions or the tie-in between
semiotic and social structures. Of course, this is somewhat
like condemning all those who died before the coming of
Christ for never getting the chance to accept Him. However
inadequate as social scientists and semioticians the editors
may have been, their own work displays that informal
expertise that is second nature to the habitué of books. The
innocence embraced by Trilling is an innocence predicated
on the expectation that the primary purpose of literature
(and criticism) is the communication of artistic vision. None
of the editors would have claimed, as does a recent adver-
tisement for the *London Review of Books*, that the club was
"unashamedly intellectual." The book club was not only
not unashamed, it was clearly in the Arnoldian mold of
bringing intellectual news to all those who were, as Arnold
observed, "interested in the advance of the general culture." Its legitimacy was fact because it remained unstated.

Which is not to say that the editors were convinced that
such a club would work. It may have been the Age of Criticism, but it was also the end of the age (naming always fore-
shadows endings), and though "literary" and "intellectual"
were still spoken of in the same breath, what guarantee was
there that a club offering good books and only good books
would find an audience? Braiding the commercial with the
intellectual has never exactly been a surefire way of getting
to the top of the publishing heap. Still, if you're going to

throw the dice – the fuzzy literary kind – better to do it when men and women of letters are actually standing around the table. In 1950, Edmund Wilson presided over the book section at the *New Yorker*; Lincoln Kirstein was the fine arts editor of the *New Republic*; and Malcolm Cowley was a contributing editor of the *Nation*. That year the *Partisan Review* had ten thousand subscribers, and, as Auden had dryly observed: "Our intellectual marines/Landing in little magazines/Capture a trend." To be sure, a few jarheads such as William Empson and Kenneth Burke were beyond the pale of the nonspecialist reader, but that still left Desmond McCarthy, Alfred Kazin, Leslie Fiedler, Mary McCarthy, Cyril Connolly, Randall Jarrell, and George Orwell (who died in 1950) as well as critics of a more pronounced academic stripe – F. O. Matthiessen, Frederick Dupee, Allen Tate, R. P. Blackmur, Cleanth Brooks, M. H. Abrams, W. Jackson Bate, and Harry Levin – all of whom wrote for places the general educated reader could visit without a graduate-school visa.

But were there enough such interested travelers? Who made up this pool of potential customers who could be enticed by Santayana's letters or the epistolary humdingers that flew between Richard Strauss and Hugo von Hofmannsthal? Not a fan of letters? Well, the club could ship you David Riesman's *The Lonely Crowd*, the *Selected Writings of Sydney Smith*, Cesare Pavese's *Diaries*, Hannah Arendt's *The Human Condition*, or a spanking new biography of the young Sam Johnson. The secret word was "eclecticism": E. M. Forster's memoir of his great-aunt, the latest translation of Molière's *Misanthrope*, George Sansom's *History of Japan*, the *Oxford History of English Literature*. All for you, all at special savings. Of course, the book club was offering more than books at reduced rates, it was granting access to highly respected critics. To put it indelicately, Barzun, Auden, and

Trilling were trading in – literally banking on – their reputations. Trilling was already the author of a classic study of Matthew Arnold and had just published *The Liberal Imagination*; Barzun had six books under his belt, including *Berlioz and the Romantic Century*; and Auden, too, had a sizable body of work behind him, including *The Age of Anxiety* and *Nones*. Discerning readers joined the Readers' Subscription for the same reason they shopped at the neighborhood butcher instead of the supermarket. The butcher chose and cut his own meats and offered only the marbled and most tender. You not only trusted his expertise, you felt he was looking out for you.

B y the time the Readers' Subscription reemerged as the Mid-Century Book Society in 1959, the literary climate was beginning to change. As more and more books tumbled into view, and publicity mills pumped up the volume, the Mid-Century found itself in a bind. It needed subscribers, but it didn't want to carry those nominally serious works that Dwight Macdonald dubbed "Midcult," whose proliferation, Macdonald warned, would lead to an irrevocable muddling of highbrow and middlebrow. He needn't have worried. High culture would soon relocate lock, stock, and barrels of books to the university, leaving the public arena to Midcult and later PopCult (whose significance, oddly enough, would require the erudition of these same self-exiled highbrows). But without benefit of focus groups, polling methods, and questionnaires, the editors could only speculate about the audience. How few, how fit?

In statements prompted by the incorporation of the Mid-Century Book Society, the editors attempted to identify the people they were writing for. Barzun spoke of readers who might appreciate the very books the editors would choose for themselves; Trilling spoke of those who "stand at the middle level of taste" and mentioned giving his dentist a copy of Norman O. Brown's *Life Against Death*. Auden was both more direct and more dreamy. Unlike his two confreres, he acknowledged the less-than-intellectual nature of the exercise; it was marketing strategy pure and simple. Their real rivals, Auden speculated, were not the Book of the Month Club and the Literary Guild but paperback series such as Anchor Books and Penguins, which traded in intellectual wares. Our goal, he wrote, is "to turn our members not into high-brows, but into intellectual dandies." The highbrow, apparently, belongs to a cell of intellectuals (the cell "may be only a Little Social Beast, but a Social Beast it is"), whereas the intellectual dandy is unique and opposed to cells of all kinds. This leads to a problem: How do you appeal to the person who would never dream of joining a book club in the first place? One must advertise, said Auden, and since advertising "is based on the proposition that unique persons do not exist, only social beings with socially conditioned and predictable desires," the only way of promoting the club, he counseled the front office, was:

> Be modest. Keep your voice low. Remember that you are selling books, not authors. Be brief. Be ABSOLUTELY HONEST. NEVER EXAGGERATE. Be witty if you can, but remember that nothing is more awful than a bad joke.

What was he thinking? This isn't practical advice for advertisers, although it makes good sense when reviewing books.

During the eleven years that they wrote for the book clubs, Auden, Barzun, and Trilling turned in some 173 reviews and essays, covering novels, poetry, letters, anthologies, histories, and biographies, as well as books on natural

116

history, music, theater, the arts, society, and civilization. Some are patently book reviews; others, full-length essays. A small number began life as introductions to books; others as homages to authors alive or dead. There are solemn and not-so-solemn essays, some of an Olympian judiciousness and others of a casualness that almost borders on whimsy. In the main, they were occasional pieces, which meant that the editors' loftier concerns – Auden's religiosity, Trilling's Freudianism, Barzun's Pragmatism – were reined in. But there were also pieces occasioned simply by enthusiasm for a particular book or author, and given the editors' cosmopolitan backgrounds, neither the books nor the reviews reflect a peculiarly American bias. French, German, and English authors are touted as regularly as American ones.

Each of the editors naturally had his own "domain," yet any one of them could have stepped in for the other and, in a manner of speaking, did. If Barzun got the nod to write about Virginia Woolf's *Diaries* for the *Griffin*, Auden might turn around and review it for the *New Yorker*. The great thing was that they'd been handed a bully pulpit to write about what interested them and even, on occasion, what they had an interest in. Barzun's translation of Beaumarchais's *Marriage of Figaro* is praised by Auden, while Trilling pushes the *Poems of Cavafy*, which is published with an introduction by Auden. But at least this vested interest was out in the open; subscribers could take a recommendation or leave it. The idea behind the book club remained one of trust: if the book was good enough for the editors, it was good enough for the subscribers.

This trust was confirmed monthly by the club's publications, which in size, format, and number of pages were more like the little magazines of the day than the standard blurb-like communiqués from other book clubs. Aside from one or two reviews by the editors, you might find an article by Mark Van Doren, E. M. Forster, Saul Bellow, or Richard Poirer. In one issue of the *Griffin*, Elia Kazan reminisced about directing *A Streetcar Named Desire*; in another, Trilling's "The Early Edmund Wilson" is followed by Wilson's own "A Modest Self-Tribute." On occasion, the subscriber might stumble across a passage from Baudelaire's letters, an excerpt from Nietzsche's reflections on Schopenhauer, or a sketch by Leslie Stephen.

But it was Auden, Barzun, and Trilling the subscribers paid to read, a fact not lost on the trio. Although their literary considerations could be as short as a thousand words, the usual entry was around thirty-five hundred words. Moreover, the editors shared the work, often reading the same books and blue-penciling one another's drafts. Each had a hand in what the others wrote, but not so you'd notice more than one set of fingerprints. Auden's contributions, understandably, are the least academic in spirit; Trilling's, the most serious and reflective (except on those occasions when they're not), and Barzun's are at once plainspoken and rich in detail. A hasty generalization derived from their respective styles: Auden delights in the world and occasionally finds himself annoyed by the world in which books play a large part; Trilling is delighted or annoyed by books in which the world plays a large part; and Barzun, enamored of order but wary of systemization, seems the most comfortable in the world and in his own skin.

And all three seemed comfortable with their chosen sideline. The book club was *their* club too, where they could kick back, light up a cigarette (Auden and Trilling smoked like dragons), go through the publishers' lists or parcels of manuscripts, and divvy up the goods. Barzun gets Shaw, Proust, Montaigne, and Molière; Trilling gets Bellow, Baldwin, Dickens, and Nabokov; Auden gets Sydney Smith, Marianne Moore, John Betjeman, and Ford Madox Ford.

And we sometimes get surprises: it's not Auden who draws Kenneth Tynan's *Curtains*, but Trilling; not Trilling who wades into the Faulknerian underbrush, but Auden.

No less than his uptown accomplices, Auden had a pedagogical streak, though he pretended otherwise. "Criticism should be casual conversation," he remarked when it was suggested that he oversee a volume of his collected prose. He also liked to play down his reviewing assignments. His review of Muriel Spark's three novels begins: "It is all too easy for a reviewer to confuse his job with that of the literary critic. A reviewer must remember that his audience has not read the book which he is discussing; a critic starts with the assumption that his audience is fairly familiar with the work or author he is reexamining." No doubt this is so, but it is also more than just a matter of switching hats. Book reviewers come and go, and most of them depart without causing us undue distress. But every so often one appears who makes us want to read more of *his* work, rather than that of the writer under review. Auden may have slighted his criticism publicly, but he took it seriously. James Fenton goes so far as to say that, in Auden's work, "prose and poetry interpenetrate to a far greater extent than in the work of any other English-language poet of this century." Auden may have written prose for lucre and poetry for love, but, as Auden's executor Edward Mendelson shrewdly observes, Auden was a poet who dramatized the tension between public responsibility and private desire, whose poems speak in "the voice of a citizen who knows the obligations of his citizenship." Could his other — his prose — voice do less?

This may be the place to say that of the three editors, it is Trilling who, at times, seems the least characteristic. His vaunted prose style, commonly described by his detractors as baroque, complex, and opaque, is less in evidence here than in his other essays. Although not everyone finds his mature style troublesome, it is tough to reconcile the Trilling of the book clubs with the Trilling of the *Partisan Review*, a distinction he himself made in the preface to *A Gathering of Fugitives*, which captured (among others) a dozen of his book-club pieces. Because the club's subscribers essentially amounted to a captive audience, Trilling could say that he was led "to write less formally than I usually do, and more personally, even autobiographically. . . . Writing frequently and regularly for the same audience relaxes the manner of address." And while his penchant for going into things could not always be stifled by the quick turnaround required by monthly reviewing (witness his pieces on Lawrence Durrell's *Alexandria Quartet* and Saul Bellow's *The Adventures of Augie March*), there are also some fine examples of Trilling "light" (see "Practical Cats More Practical Than Ever Before").

Mark Krupnick makes much of this division in *Lionel Trilling and the Fate of Cultural Criticism*, characterizing him as both avant-garde intellectual ("alienated, agonized, intransigently adversary in temper") and book-club editor ("relaxed, comfortable, at ease in the world"). But why the dissection? Trilling was as much a teacher of literature as a writer, and as much a writer of literature as a critic; and all three personas showed up at the book club. In an eloquent memoir, written a year after Trilling's death in 1975, Barzun drew a connection between the book club's genesis and Trilling's intellectual makeup. When Trilling mentioned his interest in a proposal "to disseminate good books," Barzun took it in stride. He knew the man, knew that he "was not a 'humanist' against science or social science, or a 'critic' against 'scholarship.' Nor did he look down on the general public as an undifferentiated mass of barbarians: all his remonstrances were directed in the first place at professionals who could fight back."

If Trilling's prose is complicated, it is also accessible; if he seems, on occasion, indecisive, he is persuasively so. Literature worried him; it worried at him. In essay after essay, he seems to be asking, "What is it that literature depends on for its effect?" The cultural complicity of literature, about which ideologues make such a fuss, Trilling took for granted. Because culture envelops us, because even the ways we reject it are culturally determined, no judgment can be entirely devoid of a certain inquisitorial tension. This isn't ambivalence or uncertainty but the intuition that decisive formulations about art must be extracted from a mess of antinomies. "What is it that literature depends on for its effect?" Trilling's answer, or at least one variation of it, expressed in a characteristic dialectical trope, stresses both "the aesthetic effect of intellectual cogency" and "the *primitive* which is of the highest value to the literary artist." "Intellectual power and emotional power go together," he wrote in "The Meaning of a Literary Idea" — a statement that goes a long way toward explaining why aesthetic judgments are allergic to one or another theoretical blanket.

Barzun, who began to teach with Trilling in 1934, took a different approach to the complexity that all thoughtful people sense when taking stock of their surroundings. As Barzun remembers:

> Trilling was bent on developing the large consequences of the often hidden relations and implications for life that he found in literature. I was trying to compress great batches of fact and opinion into descriptions and conclusions that the reader of history could grasp. . . . The excess on my side that Lionel re-

proved was, therefore, a characteristic unwillingness to "go into it." Some decisive formulation of mine would make him curious, raise his antennae for the complex, and he would say, "Open it up – that sentence deserves a paragraph . . . that paragraph, a page."

But whether it is Barzun's shorter, more direct sentences, Auden's elegantly casual prose, or Trilling's undulating elaborations, it is ultimately the high state of awareness each brought to the work that repays our investment.

Civic-minded criticism is neither moralizing sentiment nor sermonizing cant. Criticism is an aid, not an answer; and the book club, as envisioned by its board, exemplified a tending-to-the-flock mentality, shepherding readers, so to speak, toward nutritious leaves of grass. In more urban terms, the editors, albeit self-appointed, were the public's proxy, investing its capital in literary markets that would pay out. They may not always have walked a fine line between high-handed and high-minded, but in writing for the general educated public they wrote as themselves, not as a committee, and certainly not in the service of any one ideological cause. Matthew Arnold would have approved. In a little-known essay, "The Bishop and the Philosopher," Arnold noted that there are some books, however specialized or scholarly, that seem to require the critic's attention, for the obvious reason that not everyone "is a theologian or a historian or a philosopher, but everyone is interested in the advance of the general culture." He may have been reaching, but even if there was only one interested party, it would be enough to justify the critic's intervention. The book Arnold had in mind was one of biblical scholarship, a subject in which he lacked the requisite academic credentials. But as he explained, "[A] work of this kind has to justify itself before another tribunal." The editors *were* that tribunal, and the book club was their excellent Arnoldian adventure.

In retrospect, there was something wonderfully optimistic about the whole enterprise. Perhaps it's because we live in a time when literature is pinioned by criticism and overshadowed by media that the first meeting of the Readers' Subscription Book Club begins to blend with one of those MGM movies in which Judy Garland and Mickey Rooney get the bright idea of putting on a show. This is not to suggest that the book club wasn't serious; it certainly was, but the boys were having fun and they let you know it. They were like those classical musicians who, on leaving work at the symphony, head downtown to play jazz all night in a smoky club. Did they go downtown on books? In a loose sense, yes – not during every set, of course, but every so often one or another of the trio would launch into an uncharacteristic riff that signaled the pleasure they derived from playing together; and surely no small part of that enjoyment lay in the knowledge that they were performing for a literate audience who had come expressly to hear them.

No Failure
Like Success

The Life of Raymond Chandler

AROUND THE TIME a transplanted adolescent American was matriculating at the Dulwich College Preparatory School in South London, studying music, divinity, and the classics, a peculiar American form of reading entertainment known as the "pulps" was just getting off the ground. Printed on seven by ten inches of untrimmed wood pulp, featuring sensationalistic fiction and even more fantastic ads, the pulps soon enthralled a nation of readers – or at least those who liked their women fast and their action faster. Had the youngster at the Dulwich School been aware of those first pulps, the *Argosy* (1896) and *All-Story* (1905), which soon called forth a hundred sexy and snarling imitators, no doubt he would have sniffed and returned to his Ovid and Thucydides, which he was reading in Latin and Greek. In other words, it would have taken a wily Nostradamus with a piquant sense of humor to predict that this product of an English public school education would one day place his stamp on a gaudy, lowbrow form of writing and make it, as he put it, "into something like literature."

That modest, but not-too-modest, appraisal has now been shored up – one might even say raised up – by the Library of America's decision to reprint the works of Raymond Chandler.

Coming at a time when the distinction between high culture and popular culture is vaguer than ever, and when the time-bound views of fallible human beings who happen to be writers are adduced to the detriment of their actual achievement, the Library of America's inclusion of Raymond Chandler presents an interesting case. Enemies of elitism will cheer, but since they are for the most part the same professors who unearth politically incorrect views in everyone from Lucretius to Lincoln, they will not find Chandler fighting the good fight, at least not where African Americans, Native Americans, Jews, and homosexuals are concerned. Possibly the Library's decision was purely literary: someone or some committee evidently felt that Chandler belongs in the company of Lincoln, Twain, Hawthorne, Melville, Wharton, James, Faulkner, and Frost.

Chandler, in case one is an immitigable highbrow and disdains to know such things, wrote fiction almost exclusively from the vantage point of a California private eye. He also worked on half a dozen screenplays and published exactly five essays. Given that we are speaking of some two dozen short stories (many of them fairly weak) and only seven novels, the question must be asked: Does Chandler belong in any literary pantheon that is not restricted to mystery or detective fiction? Or to put it another way: Would a mystery writer at any other time but ours be considered for literary sanctification?

Writers, mystery buffs, and even many educated readers of detective fiction will tell you that Chandler is a wonderful writer, not a great *genre* writer mind you, but a great writer. Readers with less than a personal investment in detective fiction will shrug off such an exalted notion. Flaubert or Joyce, he's not. But he is a fine stylist, a craftsman who labored to fashion an original prose style whose precision and panache, often imitated, has never been duplicated. The best of Chandler looks down on the imitations like an old master portrait hanging among thousands of family snapshots.

Of course, if you don't have an eye for these things or a tolerance for the hardboiled detective tale, you may not discern the difference or care about it – in which case, the Library of America's imprimatur will count for little. Skeptics, however, should note that Chandler, despite an ambivalence second to none regarding crime fiction, took his work seriously, believing he could rehabilitate a shabby stylistic cousin of standard English. The prose tradition he inherited – one finally shorn of its British roots – sprang directly from American print journalism and the story weeklies and dime novels of the late nineteenth century. Although the private eye's antecedents may be found in James Fenimore Cooper's *Leatherstocking Tales* and Mark Twain's pungent first-person narratives, a far more generative condition for the pulps was the demand for plentiful prose delivered in record time – which, it hardly needs saying, tended to produce literary effects appealing to a broad and uncritical readership. Ludwig Wittgenstein may have eagerly awaited his monthly issue of Street & Smith's *Detective Story Magazine*, but then Ludwig was as an odd duck as well as a genius. In truth, few middlebrow readers, let alone intellectuals, ever gave the pulps a glance.

So along comes Raymond Thornton Chandler (1888–1959) – Chicago born, Nebraska raised, and England educated – to give such writing a veneer of respectability. He did not alter general opinion about the pulps (they were pretty dreadful, and Chandler said so), but he did manage to take a genus of pulp writing, the hardboiled detective story, and invest it with a rude wit and wised-up intelligence that made even readers of serious literature sit up and take notice. Yet in satisfying the reading public, Chandler would end up disappointing himself. However much he railed at the arbitrary distinctions that separated "straight" fiction from detective fiction, Chandler would have preferred to go straight.

Fully prepared to take up a business career after leaving Dulwich, Chandler qualifies for a job in the supplies office of the Admiralty in 1907. He lasts all of six months. For the next two years he works sporadically for English newspapers while writing poems, sketches, and book reviews on the side. In 1911 he manages to place a few literary essays in the *Academy*. A year later, unable to earn money by writing, he throws in the towel. With five hundred pounds borrowed from an uncle, Chandler returns to America, where, after knocking around a bit, picking apricots and stringing tennis rackets, he becomes an accountant for the Los Angeles Creamery.

In 1917 he enlists in the Canadian Army and sees action in France. Two wartime experiences stand out: he is the sole survivor of a German artillery bombardment and, as platoon leader, has the responsibility of leading his men into machine-gun fire. After the war, Chandler returns to Los Angeles and meets Pearl Eugenie ("Cissy") Pascal, a married woman eighteen years his senior. During their affair, his mother drops in, stays on, and Chandler takes a job as an auditor for an oil company. After his mother's death, Chandler marries the now-divorced Cissy (he is thirty-six; she, fifty-four) and quickly works his way up to vice president in charge of the L.A. office.

The next seven years find him working hard, drinking heavily, dallying with other women, and occasionally displaying erratic behavior. In 1932 he is fired. With nothing to do, Chandler again tries to write. This time, however, he eschews poetry and essays for the pulps because it has occurred to him that he might like to be paid for writing.

Five months of work and he produces his first detective story, which is accepted by *Black Mask* (1933), the best pulp magazine of the day (started by, of all people, H. L. Mencken). More stories follow, and in 1938 he finishes *The Big Sleep*, the novel that effectively launches his literary career and, just as effectively, prohibits a life in literature as he had once envisioned it.

Chandler's travails have been nicely recounted in Frank MacShane's *The Life of Raymond Chandler*, which has the admirable quality, rare these days, of being both informative and brief. Without drumming the point home, MacShane also suggests that, given Chandler's grounding in the classics, his youthful literary aspirations, and his unswerving romanticism, the fact that he ended up writing hardboiled detective fiction was, despite his worldly success and its acclaimed brilliance, something of an intellectual cross for him. From the moment he began to publish, Chandler veered from dismissive remarks about his work to grandiose pronouncements about how well it stacked up against the "straight" fiction of the day. Always contemptuous of popular mystery novels, especially the British "cozy," Chandler managed to convince himself that good "murder novels ... are no easier reading than *Hamlet*, *Lear*, or *Macbeth*. They border on tragedy and never quite become tragic. Their form imposes a certain clarity of outline which is only found in the most accomplished 'straight' novels." Of course, if a critic gave too much weight to his own work, he was immediately suspicious. When W. H. Auden pronounced Chandler to be "interested in writing, not detective stories, but serious studies of a criminal milieu," Chandler demurred: "Auden leaves me lost and groping. . . . I'm just a fellow who jacked up a few pulp novelettes into book form." Not to like his work was to misunderstand it; to like it too much was to overestimate it. "The better you write a mystery," he informed his London publisher, "the more clearly you demonstrate that the mystery is not really worth writing."

The sense of doing something well that may not be worth doing at all never left him. The same classical education that helped him to write clean, economical sentences made him painfully ambivalent toward the form that summoned them. He regarded writing detective fiction as an architect might feel toward designing useless, elaborate boxes. On the other hand, Chandler also felt that his boxes had to be rendered perfectly. He analyzed, parsed, imitated, and revised repeatedly, teaching himself to write pulp stories, as MacShane notes, "in the same spirit as translating Cicero into English and then back into Latin" – which is just what he had done at Dulwich.

The other difference between Chandler and even competent pulp writers was an ear trained in Edwardian England. "I had to learn American just like a foreign language," he said, and certainly that played into the hands of a writer who believed that "the most durable thing in writing is style, and style is the most valuable investment a writer can make with his time."* From the outset, Chandler thought he

---

* Fredric Jameson makes rather too much of this: "Language can never again be unself-conscious for him; words can never again be unproblematical." Certainly Chandler's distance from the American vernacular gave him a different slant on it, but when is language not problematical? All style is self-conscious and, as Chandler noted, "a projection of personality." Style is not so much about the self as it is about the self that writes, though in some cases the difference is not immediately apparent.

could do things with detective fiction that readers didn't even know they wanted. "They just *thought* they cared nothing about anything but the action," he claimed.

130

> The things they really cared about, and that I cared about, were the creation of emotion through dialogue and description; the things they remembered, that haunted them, were not for example that a man got killed, but that in the moment of his death he was trying to pick a paper-clip up off the polished surface of a desk.

Much the same point, incidentally, is made in F. Scott Fitzgerald's *The Last Tycoon* when studio executive Monroe Stahr, using a nickel rather than a paper clip, expatiates on the art of writing for the movies.

Like its maker, Chandler's famous style contains a contradiction. Although he admired Dashiell Hammett for giving murder back to the nasty, impulsive people who commit it and who "talk and think in the language they customarily used for such purposes," Chandler was not about to get realistic. Hammett, though no stranger to Gothic plotting, wrote matter-of-factly. But then Hammett was the real article – he'd been a Pinkerton detective and hung out with cops and robbers, saloon owners and such – and perhaps felt no need to embellish. Chandler, on the other hand, learned about criminals from newspapers, textbooks, and the pulps. Both physically and temperamentally removed from the rough-and-tumble, he had to find a way to get himself interested in writing about it. "How could I possibly care a button about the detective story as a form?" he explained to the editor of *Harper's*.

> All I'm looking for is an excuse for certain experiments
> in dramatic dialogue. To justify them I have to have
> plot and situation; but fundamentally I care almost
> nothing about either. All I really care about is what
> Errol Flynn calls "the music," the lines he has to speak.

Chandler was not being disingenuous, but music was not all he cared about. He would also claim with typical contrariety that had essays paid enough, he would have given up fiction altogether. One may doubt it; fiction freed him – his character Philip Marlowe freed him – to sing of chivalric quests (this, after all, was a writer who never quit dabbling with poetry and fabulistic tales); at the same time, Marlowe also enabled him to express the bitterness and disillusionment of a man coming to maturity in the period between the wars.

One forgets that Chandler was part of the Lost Generation, one of the writers who emerged from the trenches intact in limb only. "A sense of wrong" pervades his writing, observes Jacques Barzun, a conviction that "society, mankind is corrupt – all but a few scattered individuals." Marlowe is society's antithesis, immune to the temptations of money, power, and flesh – the one incorruptible individual. Much as one is tired of seeing Chandler's famous definition of the detective reprinted, and much as one would like to forgo any mention of it, it can't be done. Marlowe is the Hamlet of private eyes, not because more has been written about him than about any other shamus or because he is cynical, sentimental, and even, on occasion, somewhat hysterical on the subject of women, but because we think we know him better than he knew himself.

> But down these mean streets a man must go who is not
> himself mean, who is neither tarnished nor afraid. . . .

He is the hero, he is everything. He must be a complete man and common man and yet an unusual man ... if he is a man of honor in one thing, he is that in all things. He is a relatively poor man, or he would not be a detective at all. . . . He will take no man's money dishonestly and no man's insolence without a due and dispassionate revenge. He is a lonely man and his pride is that you will treat him as a proud man or be very sorry you ever saw him. He talks as the man of his age talks, that is, with rude wit, a lively sense of the grotesque, a disgust for sham, and a contempt for pettiness.

In short, the detective is Chandler without Chandler's personal failings. It is unthinkable that Marlowe could give in to despair, behave dishonorably, contemplate suicide, or make a fool of himself over women (that was the province of his creator). Nothing fazes him, nothing can humiliate him; and like Sam Spade before him, Marlowe won't "play the sap," not even for the woman he loves. Which, of course, is what appeals to the sap in all men who must knuckle under to girlfriends, wives, and employers. Marlowe's refusal to compromise is embodied in the very language used against those who attempt to diminish him; words themselves become a mode of resistance, a verbal sock to the jaw.

The wrongness of Chandler's world is thus kept at bay by the brusque, evocative language of the books, a style that Fredric Jameson equates with an underlying attitude of distrust, "a kind of outgoing belligerence, or hostility, or the amusement of the native . . . always nuanced or colored by an attitude." And whenever Chandler's dialogue strays into "something more intimate and more expressive, it begins to falter; for his forte is the speech pattern of inauthenticity, of externality, and derives immediately from the inner organic logic of his material itself."

> "Did I hurt your head much?"
> "You and every other man I ever met."

> "I don't like your manner."
> "That's all right. I'm not selling it."

> "Who's your buddy?"
> "Big Willie Magoon. He thinks he's tough."
> "You mean he isn't sure?"

No less important than the attitude is the lonely figure of Marlowe himself. Certainly a large part of the books' appeal lies in the curious vulnerability of this wise-cracking detective. Although the private eye's solitary existence is now part of the American scene, even something of a cliché, there is something special about Marlowe's, perhaps because his voice is filtered through Chandler's own deep-rooted melancholy. "I think he will always have a fairly shabby office, a lonely house, a number of affairs but no permanent connection," Chandler mused. "I see him on a lonely street, in lonely rooms, puzzled, but never quite defeated."

Marlowe's loneliness tempers his cynicism and wit; and we read his firsthand accounts with a sympathy reserved for people we would like to have as friends. And, of course, we approve of his way with words. Just about everyone likes to quote from the first page of *Farewell, My Lovely*: "Even on Central Avenue, not the quietest dressed street in the world, he looked about as inconspicuous as a tarantula on a slice of angel food." Clive James can't get over Chandler's description of a blonde sexy enough "to make a bishop kick a hole in a stained glass window," but other readers may prefer the small, seedy touches: "There was a desk and a night clerk with one of those mustaches that gets stuck under your fingernail." Five bullets pumped into a stomach "made no more sound than fingers going into a glove." And the voice of a hungover middle-aged woman "dragged itself out of her throat like a sick man getting out of bed."

Not everyone is impressed by this. Kingsley Amis found a moral pretentiousness in Marlowe that was underlined by a corresponding stylistic pretentiousness. Of the big three – Hammett, Chandler, and Spillane – Amis preferred the last: "Few novelists on any level can match Spillane's skill in getting his essential facts across palatably and without interrupting the action." Arrant nonsense. Bad writing by itself is sufficient to stop the action, and Spillane is 95 percent bad writing. In Amis's preference for honest bad writing over attempts to ennoble or solemnize the hard-boiled tale, there is a perverse snobbism at work; like some Regency aristocrat, Amis disdains middle-class pastimes for the low amusement of bare-knuckle boxing.

Chandler is also not a favorite of writers such as James Ellroy, who himself tends to compose brooding crime tales in a staccato, hyperventilated mode. "I see hardboiled crime fiction as a heavily ritualized transit horseshit and largely spun off of Raymond Chandler," Ellroy groused. "Chandler is a very easy writer to imitate, which is why so many people have been able to adapt his formula with such success, but I hate that formula, and I hate its sensibility." More nonsense. Hating Chandler's sensibility is one thing, but he is almost impossible to imitate. There has been precious little good tough-guy detective fiction written since Chandler's day: James Crumley's *The Last Good Kiss*; Andrew Bergman's *The Big Kiss-Off of 1944*; Timothy Harris's *Kyd for Hire*, and parts of Robert B. Parker's Spenser novels come to mind. But the vast majority of hard-boiled books are awful stuff indeed. What's astonishing is not the poor quality of the imitations but that Chandler has not spoiled more readers. You'd think that people, reviewers included, could discern the difference between chuck and prime – speaking of which, S. J. Perelman's parody "Farewell, My Lovely Appetizer" reminds us that good hard-boiled fare is more than just a matter of gats and gams.

If Chandler had been a mannerist only, how do we account for the number of serious critics – Auden, Maugham, Barzun, Edmund Wilson, Jameson, and Geoffrey H. Hartman – who addressed the work long before there was anything like popular culture studies? Now, of course, when everything from billboards to court records is seen to possess social and semiotic relevance, the hard-boiled formula is not merely a serviceable literary device. No indeed; it is, according to one specialist, "an escape from the full implications of the modern naturalistic moral universe . . . an escape from the naturalistic consciousness of determinism and meaningless death just as it embodies a flight from the other-directed anxiety about success and conformity." This is what you get when you train a howitzer on a birdhouse.

One thing the popular culturalists get right is the role of the city in these stories, though they are not the first to have noticed. In 1902 G. K. Chesterton found the detective story to be

the earliest and only form of popular literature in which is expressed some sense of the poetry of modern life. . . . No one can have failed to notice that in these stories the hero or the investigator crosses London with something of the loneliness and liberty of a prince in a tale of elf land, that in the course of that

> incalculable journey . . . [t]he lights of the city begin
> to glow like innumerable goblin eyes, since they are
> the guardians of some secret, however crude, which
> the writer knows and the reader does not.

136

I don't wish to dispute the mind that created the mind of Father Brown, but an addendum is in order. While Auguste Dupin may have pounded the Parisian pavements looking for purloined letters and bad-tempered orangutans, and Sherlock Holmes fraternized with the denizens of London's underclass, it is only when the upper-class investigator metamorphoses into the private eye that the detective truly becomes one with the city. It's no accident that the first private eyes – John Carroll Daly's Race Williams and Hammett's Continental Op – emerged at a time when city governments were intent on collecting power, and racketeers on collecting city governments. In the 1920s, American cities had become, in Auden's phrase, the "Great Wrong Place," open all night and to all social classes, the perfect place to hide missing heiresses, misfits, and murderers.

As students of the mystery genre know, murder in the country was a snake in the garden, a disruption of the pastoral order, whereas violence in cities was the natural order. In the countryside, with its rigid class structure, the victim and executioner were often related, while in the anonymous urban landscape, in which people were free to reinvent themselves, murder often occurred as a by-product or accident; victim and murderer often strangers. The right man in the wrong place was the peeper, shamus, gumshoe, dick – a man able to ferret out secrets and past identities – for whom neither the city's glamour nor its sordidness could hide the naked ambitions, faded hopes, elaborate lies, or the corruption that stretched from the dockyard slums to the mansions on the hill.

We curved through the bright mile or two of the Strip, past the antique shops with famous screen names on them, past the windows full of point lace and ancient pewter, past the gleaming new night clubs with famous chefs and equally famous gambling rooms, run by polished graduates of the Purple Gang, past the Georgian-Colonial vogue, now old hat, past the handsome modernistic buildings in which the Hollywood flesh-peddlers never stop talking money.... Past all this and down a wide smooth curve to the bridle path of Beverly Hills and lights to the south, all colors of the spectrum and crystal clear in an evening without fog, past the shadowed mansions up on the hills to the north, past Beverly Hills altogether and up into the twisting foothill boulevard and the sudden cool dusk and the drift of wind from the sea.

(Farewell, My Lovely)

Although this passage is coated with a residue of *Gatsby*-like lushness, it's good writing in anyone's book, and there is enough of it throughout Chandler's novels to warrant Auden and Co.'s thinking more of Chandler's work than he did himself. And while *The High Window* and *The Little Sister* are marred by overplotting and digressions, and parts of *The Long Goodbye* are too long by half, much of Chandler's fiction remains fresh and funny sixty years after its inception.

Chandler, in my experience, is the only writer of thrillers whose novels literary types and intellectuals could read above the bedcovers (nowadays that honor has fallen upon Elmore Leonard and Ross Thomas). Yet no matter how much we liked him, we still didn't know where he fit in. In short, we felt the same ambivalence toward his work that Chandler himself and such subtle critics as Desmond MacCarthy also felt. But if there is less to Chandler than the popular culturalists would have us believe, there is more to him than dismissive highbrows would like to believe. And what both often miss is the sheer good humor of the writing, especially in the stories and early novels, which include scenes bordering on self-parody, as well as dialogue that only a man enjoying himself could write.

> The kid said: "I don't like drunks in the first place, and in the second place I don't like them getting drunk in here, and in the third place I don't like them in the first place."
> "Warner Brothers could use that," I said.
> "They did."

Like other certified melancholics – Swift and Dr. Johnson, to name two – Chandler depended on humor and a sense of the grotesque to get by. Marlowe's voice was the work of a particular mood: irreverence, impudence, and gusto combining to produce the deft descriptions, outrageous similes, and bright repartee that constitute Chandler's narrative at its best. But no matter how good the writing – and Chandler knew when it was good – nothing could shake the conviction that he was working not only in a mediocre field, but a foreign one as well. A point poignantly brought home when Alfred Knopf sent him a book by Max Beerbohm. Chandler wrote back: "I found it sad reading. It belongs to the age of taste, to which I once belonged. It is possible that like Beerbohm I was born half a century too late, and that I too belong to an age of grace. I could so easily have become everything the world has no use for. So I wrote for *Black Mask*. What a wry joke."

After the success of *The Big Sleep*, Chandler followed up with possibly the purest of the novels in terms of plotting, humor, and snappy dialogue, *Farewell, My Lovely*, which even Edmund Wilson, who flared his fastidious nostrils at the formal detective story, conceded contained good writing. Did this make Chandler happy? Of course not. Wilson was just "a fat bore" who in the *Memoirs of Hecate County* had managed to make "fornication as dull as a railroad time table." Other than Cissy, very little seemed to perk Chandler up. And Cissy was growing old, making the age difference between them increasingly evident. Nor did his disposition improve when he began working for the movie studios in 1943. His collaboration with Billy Wilder on the screenplay of *Double Indemnity*, and with Alfred Hitchcock on *Strangers on a Train*, turned out to be unpleasant experiences for all involved. Bad times and good money are a recipe for boozing, and Chandler's health began to fail. By 1949 he was suffering from bronchitis, skin allergies, and shingles – ailments that would become chronic.

At this point, Cissy developed respiratory problems and was in and out of hospitals for the rest of her life. Somehow Chandler managed to finish *The Long Goodbye*, certainly the most somber and affecting of his books, while worrying over and ministering to his aged wife. When Cissy died in the winter of 1954, Chandler was distraught. To his London publisher Hamish Hamilton, he wrote: "For thirty years, ten months and four days, she was the light of my life, my whole ambition. Anything else I did was just the fire for her to warm her hands at. That is all there is to say."

Although Chandler would live another four and a half years, he never truly recovered from Cissy's death. At loose ends, he traveled back and forth between America and England, taking up with various women he decided needed looking after. Self-pity and nostalgia envelop him; gusto and impudence take a holiday; and his last novel, *Playback*, is a testament to depression. The tone is wrong: personal but not authentic (as if Chandler and Marlowe are vying for control); and in a form that is intrinsically artificial, it is sincerity that rings false. "How can a such a hard man be so gentle?" the heroine asks. "If I wasn't hard, I wouldn't be alive," Marlowe replies. "If I couldn't ever be gentle, I wouldn't deserve to be alive." It's writing that Chandler himself might have mocked fifteen years earlier.

140

The end of Chandler's life was a sad business. His drinking again assumed heroic proportions, leading to the same erratic behavior that had marked his days in the oil business. He behaved badly with friends and publishers; he trusted people he had no reason to trust; and he became infatuated first with Natasha Spender (the poet's wife), then with his own secretary, and finally with his British agent Helga Greene. While engaged to Greene, Chandler, still drinking heavily, developed pneumonia. He died on March 26, 1959. Seventeen people attended the funeral.

A writer's life is not a stencil placed over the work, yet the dichotomy is always starkest when the work centers on a fictional alter ego who seems to compensate for the writer's own inadequacies. Readers familiar only with the novels may thus find Chandler's sensibility, as expressed in the letters, something of a surprise. Chandler's no-nonsense insights into his own and others' books show a mind relentlessly at work: expostulating on craft, explaining his intentions, and complaining when critics missed the point. No other genre writer, I suspect, took such pains both to justify the work and to distance himself from it. To read the letters is to realize that letters were as necessary to Chandler as fiction; that, in fact, one reason he wrote letters was to differentiate himself from that fellow who wrote detective novels. For it was in the letters that Chandler finally became what he had always aspired to – that is to say, a Man of Letters.

This is not lost on his biographer. His letters, MacShane notes, "are like the conversation of a man sitting by the fireplace, pondering and exploring everything he could not encompass in his fiction." Sadly, few of the letters were to intimates or other writers. Most seem to have been prompted by publishers, editors, or strangers asking for clarification. But they are personal in the best sense. Chandler seemed to communicate fearlessly, without thought of embarrassment to himself or his correspondent. The letters are thoughtful, defensive, cranky, occasionally pompous, yet always intelligent, always honest. If at times he comes off like a schoolmaster or peevish owl, how admirable, then, that the owl should have created such a credible eagle!

No, Chandler was not Marlowe, and that's the beauty of it. For readers, anyway. Authors, however, must suffer their creations when they enter the popular mind, as Arthur Conan Doyle learned to his dismay. Inevitably compared to his Baker Street sleuth, Doyle, on one occasion, got off a fine retort: "Pray get this into your cerebral tentacle: the doll and its maker are seldom identical." Chandler, responding to similar probing, took a different tack:

> Yes, I am exactly like the characters in my books. I am very tough and have been known to break a Vienna roll with my bare hands. I am very handsome, have a powerful physique, and I change my shirt regularly every Monday morning. . . . I am thirty-eight years old and have been for the last twenty years. I do not regard myself as a dead shot, but I am a pretty dan-

gerous man with a wet towel. But all in all I think my
favorite weapon is a twenty-dollar bill.

A man with a droll sense of humor is often a man capable of
recognizing his own foibles and finding humor in them. So
what do we make of Marlowe's references to homosexuals
and non-Caucasians as "fag," "queer," "nigger," "shine,"
"dinge," "Mex," "Jap," and "wetback"? The first thing to
say is that they pop up less often than some bilious critics
insinuate; and second, if you don't allow a writer to be a
man of his time, you're not giving him room to be a writer
at all. Was Chandler a bigot? He was certainly insensitive in
his choice of words, even though these were the words that
best conveyed how the people he wrote about spoke. Being
fond of England did not stop him from dropping a "limey"
now and then. But what do we make of "fat greasy sensual
Jew" or "a big burly Jew with a Hitler mustache"? Confronted with the charge of anti-Semitism, Chandler stood
his ground: "I demand the right to call a character called
Weinstein a thief without being accused of calling all Jews
thieves." A member of the Hollywood community, Chandler
knew his fair share of Jews and obviously had thought
about them:

> They want to be like everyone else, undistinguish-
> able from everyone else, except that they want to be
> Jews to themselves, and they want to be able to call
> non-Jews by the name of Gentiles. But even then they
> are not happy, because they know very well you can't
> insult a man by calling him a Gentile, whereas you
> can insult him by calling him a Jew. As long as this is
> so I don't see how you can expect the Jews not to be
> oversensitive, but at the same time I don't see why I

142

should be so unnaturally considerate of this oversensitiveness as never to use the word Jew.

The last word on the subject should not be words but actions. While living in La Jolla, Chandler refused to join the local country club. He refused because the club was restricted.

The question always comes back, as it must, to one of gravitas. It was *the* question in Chandler's life, a question that gnawed at him until the end.

> People are always suggesting to writers of my sort, "You write so well why don't you attempt a serious novel." By which they mean Marquand or Betty Smith. They would probably be insulted if one suggested that the aesthetic gap, if any, between a good mystery and the best serious novel of the last ten years is hardly measurable on any scale that could measure the gap between the serious novel and any representative piece of Attic writing of the Fourth Century B.C., any ode of Pindar or Horace or Sappho, any Chorus of Sophocles, and so on.

Such protestations are not persuasive. The gap between popular and serious fiction is not as narrow as Chandler claims; and one can't help thinking that Chandler knew this and was afraid of attempting to bridge that gap. As long as he confined himself to stylish detective fiction, as long as he was just a guy who "jacked up a few pulp novelettes into book form," he could be safe from serious scrutiny.

But the Library of America has ordained otherwise. If

one is both serious about literature and a fan of Philip Marlowe, the question of the books' literary merit cannot be avoided. The easy answer is to qualify Auden's determination that Chandler's books "should be read and judged, not as escape literature, but as works of art." That is, we might say that only as escape literature do the novels work as art. What is the crime in thinking there is art to escape literature? In which case, artificiality and frivolousness can be both tolerated and justified.

I prefer, however, a more elusive, less satisfying answer, one that accepts Chandler on his own terms as someone who took "a mediocre form and [made] something like literature out of it." Something like literature is to the canon what Louis Armstrong, Frank Sinatra, or the Beatles is to the classical repertoire. There is genius, after all, in good popular culture, and surely some wacky minor demon ("genius" originally referred to a supernatural entity) smiled upon Irving Berlin, Fred Astaire, and Little Richard. A more senior demon obviously guided Chaplin and Keaton, and if you can't spot the imp, then maybe that high brow is getting in the way of your vision.

This is not exactly granting Chandler major status, and indeed no serious critic has considered Chandler's recent canonization without putting invisible quotation marks around the word – an understandable qualification, since the word is all but unnecessary when referring to writers who were canonical before the Library of America tagged them for membership. If forced, I suppose I, too, would have to concede that Chandler is best read before one has erected a critical citadel and when one is still young enough to believe in the possibility of a man like Marlowe.

But then I am not inclined to be impartial. The more I know of the man, the more I appreciate the artistry of the writer. Could Chandler have chosen a form of writing less suited to his own temperament and sensibility? Chandler therefore becomes interesting by virtue of having created Marlowe, and vice versa – a reciprocity not shared by Poe and Dupin; Hammett and Spade; Rex Stout and Nero Wolfe; Dorothy Sayers and Lord Peter Wimsey; or Spillane and Mike Hammer. Critics who exploit the differences between Chandler and his invention seem blind to the fact that Marlowe exists only because Chandler did. (Does it need saying that a man like Marlowe would never have written about a man like Marlowe?) And yet it's not as if Marlowe sprang from whole cloth. If the prickly, unprepossessing writer doesn't compare favorably to his well-built, indomitable private eye, let's not forget that Chandler had been a soldier and later ran an oil company. True, he lived with his mother for a long time and married a much older woman, but if it was mothering he desired, he chose badly. According to MacShane, Cissy was a knockout when she and Chandler met, and photographs bear this out. It seems that as a young woman in New York, Cissy had posed nude; she also liked to houseclean in the nude. Does this sound like Mom?

In the end, it is about the work. T. J. Binyon, the biographer of Pushkin and the *Times Literary Supplement*'s mystery maven, noted years ago that the second paragraph of *The Big Sleep* brings together Hammett and Fitzgerald. I think we can take this further. Just about all of Chandler's fiction is the fruit of this union. It may not have been deliberate, but now it seems entirely natural that an incurable romantic who took his literary cue from the pulps should express the cynicism and disillusionment of his age in a stylistically rich, comedic artifice, where language reigns supreme. "I live for syntax," Chandler said, and we should take him at his word. Not melancholy or alcoholism or numerous infirmities distracted him from the work. And it would be wrong of us to let this love for language and dedication to craft go unheralded.

146

Here's Looking
at You

M EN OF GENIUS are not quick judges of character,"
observed Max Beerbohm. "Deep thinking and high imagining blunt that trivial instinct by which you and I size people up" "You and I" is right, Max. I'm always sizing people
up on first acquaintance – a nose, a mouth, a forehead, and
my trivial instinct swings into action. I'm not proud of this
tendency, but at least I have the guts to admit it. One look at
my jawline and you'd know this about me. Anyway, there's
nothing wrong with making snap judgments. Didn't Oscar
Wilde say that "it is only shallow people who do not judge
by appearances"? Oscar, as usual, was dead on. We, the
unshallow, run roughshod over people who think they can
fool us, who think we can't tell what they're like from the
curl of their lip or flare of their nostril. I remember the first
time I took a long, hard look at my uncle Alfred's brown
eyes and said to myself: "Watch out, this guy will steal the
wax out of your ears if you're not careful."

And it's not as if Oscar and I are in the minority. The practice of drawing connections between physical appearance

and moral character, or physiognomy, has a long and distinguished history. The ancient Egyptians believed that portrait-statues of the pharaohs had to resemble the great men themselves, so that the *Ka*, or spirit of the dead, could recognize them. Aristotle considered the face to be the index to the mind and wrote several treatises on the subject. Having noted that large ears sprout on men prone to irrelevancy, he also wondered if a passing resemblance to animals might not lead to piggish or leonine behaviors.

Aristotle's good name notwithstanding, physiognomy did not immediately become a legitimate discipline, but remained for centuries a branch of folk wisdom, the sort of thing you learned from a superstitious grandmother, like divining signs or reading palms and moles. People may have believed that appearance and behavior were related, but writers tended to see the forest rather than the trees. Epic poems and medieval romances generally ignored physical particulars, except insofar as a fair complexion marked someone as virtuous, and dark hair indicated a pagan or a traitor. Beauty was associated with goodness, but it would have been difficult to say exactly why Helen and Aphrodite were considered beautiful.

Painters also seemed content to avoid specifics, focusing instead on a formal and generic presentation of the face. This undoubtedly had less to do with the artist's skills or inclinations than with his place in society. The first portraitists were hired to do a job: to represent the lump of flesh before them in the best possible light; and since the subject was invariably a person of power and property, artists understood their role. An accurate likeness was not nearly as important as the sitter's approval – so portraitists naturally played down the grossness of the features and imbued their subjects with a benign uniformity of appearance.

And then came Leonardo.

When Leonardo looked at a face he saw differences, and he depicted these differences with an unprecedented, almost ferocious attention to detail. Although he dismissed "false physiognomy" in his *Treatise on Painting*, he allowed that the face gives "some indication of the nature of men, their vices and complexions." The indentations that separate cheeks from lips, nostrils from nose, and sockets from eyes indicated cheerfulness, while the horizontal lines on the forehead and those between the eyebrows denoted sorrow. The closer he looked, the less uniform faces became. Regarding noses alone, Leonardo enumerated ten kinds in profile, eleven in full face.

During the Renaissance, social conventions governing the relationship between artist and sitter began to change, and portraits began to register what the artist saw. But it wasn't until the publication in 1775 of Johann Kaspar Lavater's *Physiognomische Fragmente zur Beförderung der Menschenkenntniss und Menschenliebe* (hereafter referred to as the *Fragmente*) that people would learn what artist's renderings indicated. Lavater, a cultivated Swiss theologian and portrait collector, intended to persuade both artist and public that a portrait was nothing less than "the art of presenting, on the first glance of an eye, the form of a man by traits, which it would be impossible to convey by words." His elaborately detailed four-volume work argued not only that physiognomic evaluations were empirically sound but that specific faces were *anatomically consistent* with specific behaviors. Physiognomy was nothing less than a scientific method of forecasting the characterological weather. And it wasn't just general appearance that mattered: every nook and cranny on the surface of the face possessed some psychological nuance. From eyelids to earlobes, the face was now a hieroglyph of interior proclivities and intentions.

And no one laughed – least of all Lavater's publishers. By 1810, the *Fragmente* had been translated into half a dozen languages, with no fewer than twenty English versions available. Although Lavater's star has dimmed considerably, it is hard to overstate his celebrity at the turn of the nineteenth century. Lavaterian readings of faces was no parlor game: engagements, marriages, friendships, and job appointments often turned on such interpretations. Even the theory of evolution was nearly put off course when the captain of the *Beagle* took one look at Charles Darwin's face and questioned whether the naturalist's "nose could possess sufficient energy and determination for the voyage."

A man who put his money where his distinctively shaped mouth was, Lavater applied his method to the famous dispute concerning Rubens's *Four Philosophers with a Bust of Seneca*. In Lavater's eyes, the bust was decidedly not of Seneca. For one thing, the face was so unSeneca-like. Everything about it, Lavater argued, spoke of "force and impetuosity; everything announces violent passions. . . . There is in each part separately, and in their union, a shocking coarseness and vulgarity." Whether Lavater was right about the bust hardly matters; the success of the *Fragmente* did not rest on the accuracy of its physiognomic evaluations but rather on the prevailing intellectual temper. Lavater's genius was to join physiognomy to the Enlightenment's agenda of categorizing and classifying the known world. And though physiognomy gave the impression that it shared the Enlightenment's views on individuality, in truth physiognomy didn't stress individuality so much as the inequality of individuals. Indeed, the physiognomic enterprise ended up only confirming deeply ingrained cultural attitudes.

Because members of the upper classes believed that

they should look different from their social inferiors, the "science" of physiognomy both signaled and explained the physical, as well as moral, differences between the poor and the rich, the Caucasian and the Negro, the Oxbridge Brit and anyone who wasn't an Oxbridge Brit. Thus, if you didn't know what a duke, a costermonger, a virtuous woman, or an evildoer looked like, all you had to do was pick up a magazine like *Household Words*, which, in 1854, informed the British public that "between the head of a Shakespeare or a Bacon, and that of a Newgate murderer, there is as much difference as between a stately palace standing apart and a rotting hovel in a blind alley."

Speaking of heads, no discussion of physiognomy would be complete without mentioning its close cousin, phrenology – the art of reading heads. Working from close observation, Franz Joseph Gall, a German physician, contended around 1800 that parts of the brain emerge as bumps and ridges along the skull, each small bulge bearing evidence of some characterological trait. Getting one's head examined in 1820 was no figure of speech; there were plenty of phrenologists around who would palpate and measure the bumps atop and alongside one's cranium before pronouncing judgment on a person's moral fiber. As with physiognomy, phrenology had its ardent supporters, among them the scientist and evolutionist Alfred Russel Wallace, who, in 1898, lamented his century's rejection of phrenology while confidently predicting that it would "assuredly gain general acceptance in the twentieth century."

No doubt this very thought was on the mind of the young journalist who found himself at the 1921 championship fight between the brawling Jack Dempsey and the more elegant George Carpentier. After studying the heads of the two men, the reporter promptly placed his money on Carpentier on the grounds that dolichocephalic, or long-headed, men were naturally superior to men with brachy-cephalic, or round, heads. The Frenchman hit the canvas for the second and final time in the fourth round. So much for the long heads.

In the rigidly stratified class system of Victorian England, the wholesale classification of humanity into racial and ethnic types, based in part on appearances, was considered perfectly normal. When John Ruskin pronounced that the caricatures of the swells and lowlifes that appeared in *Punch* were a "source of accurate class physiognomies," he was simply acknowledging the implicit compact that existed between artist and public. Because artists knew that they had to represent different types of people in particular ways, they chose as models those who conformed to the public's idea of what a bishop or a boxer looked like. And once rendered in oils, the portrait, in turn, strengthened the public's belief in the connection between the physical and the characterological. There was a reason – if only a biased one – that the English press depicted the cartoon Irishman with a snub or "celestial" nose (wide uplifted nostrils): everyone knew that such a nose signified a partiality for drink and debauchery.

Although Lavater himself resisted absolute formulaic correspondences – not every drooping eyelid indicated a passion for vegetables – he sincerely believed that the face, if properly read, had secrets to disclose. To press home his point, he engaged the services of artists to illustrate the *Fragmente* with drawings and profiles of famous and anonymous individuals. The book's popularity actually helped promote the silhouette, after the method of drawing devised by Etienne de Silhouette. (Goethe, it is said, fell in love with a certain Charlotte von Stein after seeing her profiled likeness.)

More important, the *Fragmente* convinced many painters that the arts of reading the face and of painting it were entwined. "A painter who is no physiognomist," wrote Diderot, "is a poor painter." And the poor painter could be held accountable. When the British artist W. Holman Hunt showed his *Finding of the Saviour in the Temple* (1854–60), the painting was criticized for being "both physiologically and phrenologically incorrect." Evidently, the figure of the young Christ displayed a forehead "more distinguished by height than breadth," thereby limiting his "perceptive faculties." To add insult to injury, Christ's abdominal region was too large (suggesting a fondness for food) and his instep was not finely arched enough for a man of his . . . breeding.

153

The artist who best embodied physiognomic concerns was William Powell Frith (1819–1909). Frith, a leader of the narrative school of painting, claimed that he "had acquired a knowledge of the character and disposition that certain features and expressions betray," a belief he put to the test in his two most famous paintings, *Derby Day* (1858) and *The Railway Station* (1862). Derby Day, then England's biggest holiday and sporting event, offered up an annual macrocosm of British society. The races at Epsom Downs, outside London, allowed people of every stripe and background to mingle freely; and to Frith's credit he got them all in – the lords, lackeys, magistrates, shopkeepers, clerks, acrobats, beggars, rogues, fashionable women, fallen women, pickpockets, and thugs. The result was a social document in oil, a scroll of recognizable types, rendered with obsessive fidelity. So great was the success of *Derby Day* that Queen Victoria, on visiting the Royal Academy, abandoned her customary practice of viewing the pictures in strict catalogue order and marched directly up to it.

Frith's reputation was made – but was he a great painter or merely a competent illustrator? To one critic, Frith was "eminent among men who paint for those who like pictures without liking art." Yet no less a tastemaker than Ruskin granted him a certain proficiency, while deploring his willingness to pander to the public's taste for "jockeys, harlots, mountebanks, and men about town." Ruskin may have had in mind the lower left foreground of *Derby Day*, where a thimble-rigger, or con-man, stands flanked by a young gent who'd just been fleeced and a strongly built man in a white hat whose likeness is that of the notorious John Thurtell (1794–1824). Thurtell had shot, beaten, and slit the throat of a solicitor he thought had cheated him at cards. But it was his swaggering air that captured the fancy of the British public. Frith assumed that Thurtell would be recognized; he also assumed that the low forehead, small eyes, thick curling lips, and prognathous jaw would immediately mark him as a criminal type. Charles Dickens, for one, would have known what Frith was up to. On seeing the plaster cast of another convicted murderer, Dickens remarked that the "style of the head and set of features ... might have afforded sufficient grounds for his instant execution, even had there been no evidence against him." No *other* evidence, Dickens means.

While painters generally welcomed Lavater's eye for detail, writers found literary portraiture somewhat more daunting. "Attempts at description are stupid," George Eliot insisted. "Who can all at once describe a human being? Even when he is presented to us we only begin that knowledge of his appearance which must be completed by innumerable impressions under differing circumstances." But if the novel was going to be realistic, the face had to be taken into account. Dickens may have spoken for all writers who embraced physiognomy – a list that includes Scott, Fielding, Balzac,

Stendhal, Hawthorne, George Sand, and Tolstoy – when he declared, "Nature never writes a bad hand. Her writing, as it may be read in the human countenance, is invariably legible, if we come at all trained to the reading of it."

The script by now is all too familiar: lips denote sensuality; foreheads, intelligence; chins, determination; eyes, trustworthiness, and so on. It's precisely because we know the physiognomic code that Margaret Mitchell gave Scarlett O'Hara green eyes and a strong chin, features that testify to her capacity for envy and endurance. In *Crime and Punishment*, Dostoevsky was quick to tell us that Raskolnikov is handsome, slender, with fine dark eyes and delicate features; in other words, he is sensitive and indecisive. Hands, too, play a part. In Max Beerbohm's curious little tale, *A. V. Laider*, the title character points to the slightness of his thumbs and pinkies, observing that they mark him as a "weak and over-sensitive man – a man without confidence, a man who would certainly waver in an emergency. Rather Hamlet-ish hands." To see Hamlet in a pair of hands? Sherlock Holmes might; to him the hands revealed not only someone's occupation or hobby, but sensibility as well. As for Sherlock himself, how *un*Sherlockian he would be, if not a lean six feet with a hawklike nose.

Most writers, let it be said, are of two minds about faces. That most sensible of men, Montaigne, best sums up the ambivalence: "The face is a weak guarantee, yet it deserves our consideration." However, neither André Gide nor Somerset Maugham wished to consider it. Many writers, in fact, opted for discretion. Homer, Marlowe, Shakespeare, and Goethe wrote about Helen of Troy, but none attempted to describe her. Joyce wisely avoids scanning Molly Bloom's features, and Hemingway likewise does not linger over Lady Brett Ashley's, though he remarks that she's "built with curves like the hull of a racing yacht." In *The Portrait of a*

Lady, Henry James introduces Isabel Archer as "a tall girl in a black dress, who at first sight looked pretty." Feeling perhaps this doesn't do her justice, James has another character refer to her as "his idea of an interesting woman." That's it. A less interesting female creation is Emma Bovary, and considering the ruckus she caused in the novel and in the French courts, one might think her face had been lovingly described. But Flaubert, who knew when a *mot* was just a *mot*, simply mentions, in passing, her hair and lips, focusing only on her hand, which lacked the "soft inflection of line in its contour." What would Beerbohm make of this?

And finally, picture, if you will, Jay Gatsby. Some friends to whom I put this request described Gatsby as being of average height with brown hair and angular features. Others thought he was tall, broad shouldered, with dark hair and a broken nose. Then again, he was on the short side, fair haired, slightly effeminate. He was gaunt. He had a muscular neck. His eyes were blue. His eyes were black. Gatsby is either the product of a police artist with Cubist leanings or is himself a wonderful literary Rorschach. How does F. Scott Fitzgerald describe him? Well, he doesn't, except to call him "an elegant young roughneck a year or two over thirty."

Like it or not, physiognomy has always made good sense to a good many sensible people. "At the corner of the street," Emerson noted, "you read the possibility of each passenger, in the facial angle, in the complexion, in the depth of his eye." No mention of the nose, but if Lavater was correct, the nose is a reliable indicator of upward mobility. Caesar, Goethe, Dr. Johnson, and the Duke of Wellington all possessed noses worthy of their accomplishments, or vice versa. Indeed, at one time a short flat nose was considered somewhat suspect. "It is morally impossible that he can rise in the world," the *Illustrated London News* of May 28, 1842, said of one unfortunate fellow. "His nose keeps him down." Even Proust, a man of great refinement, identified the nose as "the organ in which stupidity is most readily displayed."

Noses aside, one might expect that we'd have wised up by now and consigned physiognomy to the intellectual junk heap. Surely the face is more than the sum of its parts. Surely we cannot know the inner man by the outer. Faces aren't writ in stone; they change as we who regard them change. And yet when the stakes are high and the evidence uncertain, we tend to fall back on first impressions. During the espionage trial of Alger Hiss, in 1950, which involved matters of national security, William Phillips, an editor of the *Partisan Review*, was moved to wonder how much support the handsome Hiss would receive if he looked more like Peter Lorre, and his accuser, the unprepossessing Whitaker Chambers, more like Gary Cooper.

Yes, there have been skeptics. "The face, for the most part," Hazlitt mused, "tells us what we have thought and felt. . . . I cannot persuade myself that any one is a great man who looks like a fool." He then added cautiously, "In this way I may be wrong." Shakespeare was more decisive: "There's no art / To find the Mind's construction in the face." They have a right to their opinions; one look at their portraits is enough to tell you that they weren't men who went along with the crowd. But who says the crowd must be wrong? Anyway, going by appearances is a natural enough weakness. In a world where things are not always what they seem, and people often disappoint, wouldn't it be nice if the face *were* a map of the psyche? With one educated glance, we'd know whom to trust, love, fear, or elect to high office. Think of it: saints and sinners distinguishable by their kissers.

Okay, so experience teaches otherwise. Men who look

like weasels don't necessarily suck eggs, and women who look like angels can make life a living hell. But knowing this isn't the same as believing it. Deep down, where that old trivial instinct stirs, I keep sizing people up on the basis of appearances. I'm not saying I can tell a good man by the cut of his jib, but if a face doesn't "feel" right to me, I won't let it get too close to my own. My face? Oh, well, you couldn't tell what I'm like just by looking at me. For instance, I'm really much more intelligent than I look. Take my word for it.

Boxers
and
Writers

TARZAN KNEW how to box. When attacked by a great
ape, he fell into a fighting stance, jabbed with his left,
crossed with his right, thus confusing and demoralizing his
hairy opponent. No one taught Tarzan how to box; no one
had to. English gentlemen, you see, are born with such
knowledge. A preposterous conceit, certainly, though not
one that would have surprised George Bernard Shaw, who
scoffed that the upper-class Englishman, having undergone
the manly rites of flogging and fighting at public schools,
"gradually persuades himself that all Englishmen can use
their fists." Shaw knew better and even wrote a novel
about prizefighting in order "to detach it from the general
elevation of moral character with which the ordinary novelist persists in associating it."

Apart from Charles Dickens, who, he claims, knew next
to nothing about fighting, Shaw never identifies these novelists. But writers – writers with apparently nothing in common – have indeed been drawn to the sport. The earliest

recorded bouts were, in fact, fictional, part of the funeral games recounted in the *Iliad* and the *Aeneid*. After that, little is heard of the sport until James Figg declared himself the first English champion in 1719. "Professor" Figg demonstrated his prowess in a London amphitheater before the likes of Alexander Pope and Jonathan Swift, and such was his celebrity that both his business card and portrait were done by William Hogarth.

One hundred years later, Lord Byron was practicing "the noble art" at ex-champion "Gentleman" John Jackson's rooms, and William Hazlitt was attending the 1821 fight between Bill Neate and "the Gasman" Tom Hickman. The international heavyweight championship match in 1860 between the American John C. Heenan and the Englishman Tom Sayers found Dickens and William Thackeray among "the fancy" (that heterogeneous mob of toughs and swells that regularly attended prizefights). Arthur Conan Doyle wrote a half dozen tales of the ring, including the popular "The Croxley Master," and made sure that Sherlock Holmes was handy with his mitts. Even the insouciant P. G. Wodehouse put on the gloves in a story or two. Among American writers, Jack London, Dashiell Hammett, Ernest Hemingway, Nelson Algren, James T. Farrell, Ring Lardner, and Budd Schulberg have all imagined the lives of boxers.

Actually, there is something these writers share – gender, a point that needs making only because a woman has finally thrown her hat into the ring. More significantly, Joyce Carol Oates's *On Boxing* is the first extended meditation on the subject for its own sake by a notable literary figure since Shaw's "Note on Modern Prizefighting" in 1901. Most recent soundings of the sport have grown out of journalistic assignments, focusing on specific bouts or fighters. Oates's sex, then, is an issue only when she calls our attention to boxing's intrinsic masculinity. She approaches boxing as a longtime, interested observer, and, aptly enough, it's not the woman who seems at times misguided, but the writer.*

The question is not why a woman has chosen to write about the sport, but why it appeals as much to the literary as to the nonliterary sensibility. Even boxing's most ardent detractors concede its extraordinary hold on much of the populace: no one sporting event – not the Super Bowl or the final game of a World Series – generates the anticipatory thrill of a big fight. The sport deserves its cicerone, someone who feels its lure and understands both its real and imagined violence. Oates seems to fit the bill, and yet her book, while engaging when dealing with particular fights and fighters, fails in the end to explain boxing enthusiasts to themselves. The problem is one of misplaced emphasis. Oates puts boxing under a philosophical lens, increasing the magnification until the sport's borders, its defining edges, disappear. Isn't this Sartre standing over her shoulder?

> The boxer meets an opponent who is a dream-distortion of himself in the sense that his weaknesses, his capacity to fail and to be seriously hurt, his intellectual miscalculations – all can be interpreted as strengths belonging to the Other; the parameters of

---

* Although the literary writer and the journalist often meet in the arena of sports, one must distinguish between those writers drawn to boxing and those paid to report on it. The first exception to this rule was the sport's first amanuensis, Pierce Egan. Egan's five-volume *Boxiania* (1812) gives a full-fledged account of the fight game, proffering the common pugilistic wisdom, though never in the common style. Egan specialized in unnecessary EMPHASIS and faux Homeric exposition (think of a cross between James Boswell and P. T. Barnum). His work was widely read and influenced such fight buffs as Thackeray and Dickens and, a century and a half later, A. J. Liebling.

his private being are nothing less than boundless assertions of the Other's self.

When a boxer is "knocked out" it does not mean . . . that he has been knocked unconscious, or even inca-pacitated; it means rather more poetically that he has been knocked out of Time. (The referee's dramatic count of ten constitutes a metaphysical parenthesis of a kind through which the fallen boxer must pene-trate if he hopes to continue in Time.)

Boxing is evidently a more solemn business than any of us realized. Corroboration comes in the form of references to Aristotle, Spinoza, and Nietzsche (even Kafka and Emily Dickinson, of all people, are worked in). This is just plain silly. Boxing and philosophy have about as much to do with one another as tennis and theology. It's not the literary lumi-naries that Oates summons who add to our understanding, but her own Lawrentian voice: "Of course, [boxing] is prim-itive, too, as birth, death, and erotic love might be said to be primitive, and forces our reluctant acknowledgement that the most profound experiences of our lives are physi-cal events."

No one, I think, could deny this, but there is a drawback to staring at the skull beneath the skin: sometimes features in full view get overlooked. After all, much about prize-fighting is no less interesting for being obvious. In *The Manly Art*, Elliott J. Gorn, a professor of American studies, states flatly that boxing "is not about instincts or male aggressiveness; it is about values, social relationships, and culture." One can dispute the weight of the evidence Gorn brings forward, but not the historical forces themselves. Oates, on the other hand, cuts through history into myth, determined to see the "meta" in the physical: "It is the lost ancestral self that is sought, however futilely" when we watch a fight. It's hard to disprove this, but how, I wonder, does she know? Oates as fan is good reading, but Oates as oracle is – well, oracular. Either you believe or you start looking around for the nearest temple exit.

163

Oates's spiritual precursor in boxing literature is Norman Mailer, whose reportage of the first Muhammad Ali–Joe Frazier fight ("Ego," published in *Life*) and subsequent cogitations on the Ali-George Foreman match (*The Fight*) often read like morality plays. Like Oates, Mailer brings us news of boxing's hidden agenda. For Mailer, boxing is "the buried South Vietnam of America"; for Oates it is "America's tragic theater." Of course, Mailer also finds in boxing another reason to write about Mailer, and Oates ties up his obsessions rather neatly: "Mailer cannot establish a connection between himself and the boxers . . . he is forever excluded from what, unthinkingly, they represent. . . . And since the great champions of our time have been black, Mailer's preoccupation with masculinity is a preoccupation with blackness as well." Here Oates writes explicitly as a woman in recognizing both her and Mailer's exclusion from boxing's codified masculine world. And perhaps it is the woman, as much as the writer, who sees Mailer's celebration of Ali as a "lovesick lament."

The empathy Oates feels for Mailer is nowhere in evidence when she turns to A. J. Liebling's *The Sweet Science*, a favorite among the fight game's literati. Oates criticizes Liebling for his "relentlessly jokey, condescending, and occasionally racist attitude" and then partially exonerates him. Apparently, the exigencies of writing for the *New Yorker* required his articles to be "arch, broad, in [their] humor, rather like situation comedy in which boxers are 'characters' depicted for our amusement."

Oates concedes hers is a minority opinion; so it ought to be, if only because it holds Liebling up as a typical *New Yorker* writer. Liebling did not write to amuse that magazine's "genteel, affluent readership"; he wrote about what amused him. To miss this is to misread everything of Liebling's. Whether he wrote about food, Louisiana politics, the press, or boxing, Liebling's writing is of a piece, communicating his relish in doing precisely what we read him doing. An amateur boxer despite his bulk, an aficionado of the ring, a connoisseur of KOs, Liebling adopted a deadpan, hyperbolic style that managed to be both respectful and waggish. Of one fighter's punches, he remarked: "They were of a force incommensurate with their purpose." The tail end of a bout elicits this description: "Both fighters looked tired, but Moore looked mean-tired behind his whiskers, like Mephistopheles on a hot night." No one has written better about the goings-on and hangers-on at big or small fights, and few writers have matched Liebling's combination of boxing expertise and literary skill: "There was Moore, riding punches, picking them off, slipping them, rolling with them, ducking them. . . . His face, emerging at instants from under the storm of arms – his own and Rocky's – looked like that of a swimming walrus."

One boxing writer who did mean to amuse is George Plimpton. In 1959, Plimpton went three rounds with Archie Moore and, despite the kindly intercession of friends who told Moore that Plimpton was a ringer, lived to write about it. *Shadow Box*, Plimpton's account of Muhammad Ali's journey from his Pennsylvania training camp to the fight with Foreman in Zaire, is a droll and shrewd look at the personalities who make up the fight game. For Plimpton, boxing isn't life, it's about making a living, and his reportorial eye falls as often on Ali's entourage as on the boss himself.

That different writers approach boxing from different perspectives is no great surprise, and perhaps it's not surprising that literary observers eventually arrive at an analogy to dialogue. Fights develop as a series of physical and psychic overtures, in which two debaters exchange attitudes, temperaments, and philosophies, each determined to score a telling point. And because each combatant exhibits certain natural tendencies as well as learned responses, Mailer can speak of one fighter "jamming up" another fighter's rhythms. In effect, Mailer is telling us how to "listen" to a fight.

All these scribes of the scuffle — Oates no less than the others — know what goes on inside the ropes. Even George Bernard Shaw, not a name that leaps to mind when one thinks of boxing, displays a hands-on knowledge of fisticuffs. Although *Cashel Byron's Profession* is basically a novelistic exercise to get in a few digs at English institutions and English hypocrisy, it seems to support the fashionable literary theory that certain writers have been read by their precursors. Shaw's descriptions of fighters of genius, whose reactions are "as instantaneous and unconscious as the calculation of the born arithmetician," and of formidable sluggers who can "take all the hammering that genius can give them" sound remarkably like Mailer's rhapsodic valuations of Ali and Frazier.

Of course, no literary demonstration of boxing's finer points can ignore its violence, and sensible apologists do not shrink from it. A fight, after all, is two men trying to beat each other senseless, and it's precisely the violent confrontation wherein the drama unfolds. Oates alludes to this but in prose more appropriate to the journal of the Modern Language Association: "In the brightly lit ring, man is *in extremis*, performing an atavistic rite or *agon* for the mysterious solace of those who can participate only vicariously in such drama: the drama of life in the flesh." Elsewhere we read that "boxing in its greatest moments suggests the bloody fifth acts of classic tragedies, in which that mysterious element we call 'plot' achieves closure."

Is this what Jack Dempsey used to tell his patrons when they stopped by his restaurant on Forty-ninth Street? Boxing is drama – of course it's drama, and we don't need theory to help us understand it. Forgetting for the moment the principals involved, the very idea of prearranged combat embraces all contests where something greater than personal glory is at stake. In a sense, every main event harkens back to David representing the Jews, and Goliath the Philistines; to Menelaus coming on the field for the Greeks, and Paris for the Trojans; to knights-errant sporting different colors. A prizefight is one nation or neighborhood putting up its best man against the champion of its rival or enemy. This is not to suggest that mythic significance attends every fight or that boxing is part of our archetypal memory. Nevertheless, some organized matches do have a historical dimension and are part of our folklore.

Liebling touches on this folkloric aspect when he reports being tapped on the noggin by Jack O'Brien, who had been hit by Bob Fitzsimmons, who had been hit by Jim Corbett, who had been hit by John L. Sullivan, until we reach the fist of Jem Mace. Muses Liebling: "It is a great thrill to feel that all that separates you from the early Victorians is a series of punches on the nose. I wonder if Professor Toynbee is as intimately attuned to his sources." While Liebling may have felt close to old-time fighters, I suspect that for some of us they have become the stuff of legend. Those bareknuckle fighters who went fifty and sixty rounds (though rounds were marked by falls, not by minutes) seem of

heartier stock than today's ten-and twelve-round con-
tenders. Anyone who has read Nat Fleischer's *Pictorial History of Boxing* has surely come away thinking that there were
giants on this earth once, some weighing only 118 pounds:
"the Old Master" Joe Gans; "Little Chocolate" George Dixon;
"the Light of Israel" Daniel Mendoza; and "Dutch" Sam,
another Jew, who owns the distinction of having "invented"
the uppercut.

Fame has always attached to victorious boxers. Even during the years when newspapers pointedly ignored illegal
bouts, doggerel and ballads bruited the fighters' names.
Needless to say, the emerging middle class in America condemned boxing – a fact that hardly affected a fighter's reputation among the lower classes. In time, the genteel and
well-to-do, emulating earlier generations of British aristoc-
racy, came to regard boxing as a manly endeavor, good for
both body and soul. One of the founders of the Boy Scouts
of America, Ernest Thompson Seton, took heart that he had
never met a boy who would not rather be John L. Sullivan
than Leo Tolstoy. Another Ernest (Hemingway), of course,
wanted to be both.

Most fights, if truth be told, are dull affairs. The greater
excitement is in the stands. Ethnic antagonisms, racial pride,
and chauvinistic hysteria often make the violence inside the
ropes seem tame by comparison. But every so often, two
men arise with differently proportioned bodies and differently cast minds, representing different constituencies, who
capture the attention of people not normally disposed to
view a fight. Such studies in contrast – Jack Dempsey vs.
Georges Carpentier, Roberto Durán vs. Sugar Ray Leonard,
Marvin Hagler vs. Thomas Hearns – resurrect grave pugilistic questions: Will the experienced man withstand the

onslaught of the younger challenger? Will the consummate boxer defeat the relentless slugger? Can finesse sidestep brute force?

If I may be allowed an Oatesian leap: perhaps each battler embodies the interested spectator's own hopes of how the world works. Is it mindless strength and energy that govern nature, or do acquired skills and elegance count for something? In such contests, the drama doesn't lie in the possibility of a knockout but in the transaction itself. The distinction is important. For while bloodlust undoubtedly is witnessed at fights, it is really an intense curiosity that draws most people, a desire to witness the fight's unfolding and to be on hand at its resolution.

In addition, there is something refreshingly open about boxing's display of aggression. What is a fair fight but meritocracy in action? In the roped-off arena, education, social status, nepotism, and chicanery are of no avail; a man is forced to rely on nothing but his own body. Knowing this, the spectator fully expects that the better man will prevail. And perhaps because in life it isn't always the man with more ability who gets ahead, we take satisfaction in a fighter's victory. In the ring, at least, the better man (when the judges are honest) always wins.

Fighters elicit admiration by throwing into relief our own physical limitations. Writers feel this as much or more than anyone else. The imperious Shaw gushed like a schoolboy on first meeting Georges Carpentier, the European light-heavyweight champion famous for his build and Gallic good looks. Writers, too, are fans, swayed by personal loyalties and patriotic feeling. Julio Cortázar recalled that the happiest moment of his youth came when another Argentinian, Luis Firpo, knocked Jack Dempsey out of the ring, and the saddest moment when Dempsey was pushed back in.

If it sometimes seems that writers have a special affinity

for boxers, it's simply because they are in a position to publicize their thoughts; any resemblance between the two professions is purely an act of the willful imagination. The solitude of each, the putting it all on the line, the naked display of ego, and other such phrases seeking to connect the writer's lot with that of the boxer are more wistful than realistic assessments of their respective operations. Indeed, it's precisely the writer's awareness of the unbridgeable gulf between the two professions that prompts such comparisons.

The writer's insights into the boxer's psyche stem from his own ambivalence concerning the inwardness and separateness of writing. For while the boxer's life turns upon action, upon a visible struggle, the writer derives his identity from the private act of writing and the secret gathering of material. In a true sense, the writer's life is lived in order to be written about. To the mental worker, then, the boxer's time in the ring is an expression of life as raw, irreducible experience, representing an enviable unself-conscious existence where moments are not appraised for their possible transmutation into art.

Such unreflective action may therefore seem more real, more vital, than the introspective, ultimately inconclusive act of writing (as if too much awareness of living were an obstacle to living completely). Even allowing for machismo, there is something fundamentally serious in this perceived deprivation. A life divorced from the rough-and-tumble of ordinary experience may be seen not only as a lost opportunity to demonstrate physical courage, but as an absence of experience. "Every man thinks meanly of himself for not having been a soldier, or not having been at sea," observed Samuel Johnson, himself an advocate of the prize ring.

This rather sweeping generalization is probably true for many men and many writers, but it is also probably true that not everyone is haunted by such regrets. There is action and there is action. Henry James doubtless felt that a significant aspect of life — namely erotic love — was denied him, but did he mind not having been a deckhand or infantryman? Would Proust, if invited, have gone on safari with Hemingway? Dr. Johnson's dictum certainly applies to some writers — for instance, to Dr. Johnson. Why else would his mistress have noticed that "no praise ever went so close to his heart as when Mr. Hamilton called out one day upon Brighthelmstone Downs, 'Why, Johnson rides as well, for aught I see, as the most illiterate fellow in England'?"

Not so amusing, however, is the tendency of writers to see themselves in a pugilistic light, hoping perhaps that the uncomplicated esteem granted to athletes will revert to them. Hemingway felt that the crown once worn by Tolstoy belonged to him, and Mailer liked to call himself the champ of writers. Mailer, in fact, so yearned to join the boxing fraternity that he cavorted with light-heavyweight champion José Torres on the *Dick Cavett Show*. One waited in vain for Truman Capote to follow suit.

Of course, no amount of literary palaver will appease boxing's critics or transform the sport into a vocation like any other. It's not. It's a brutal business, and if a valid defense exists we must look to the boxers themselves, not because disenfranchised young men benefit from boxing (few actually do) but because once in the professional ranks they deal in a level of violence incomprehensible to outsiders. The violence they mete out is not only harsher than most civilians can fathom; it is also accommodated in certain unfathomable ways. A fighter is his body, and it is as a body that he expresses himself. At the same time, he is also curiously detached from it: a body is something to be used like a tool or worn like armor. In short, his sense of himself as something designed to deliver and accept punishment is what enables him to do – and protects him from – violence.

But however routine such violence becomes to the professional, a fight is still a nasty bit of work. It is not, as some writers like to claim, an aesthetic enactment, erotic dance, savage ceremony, or chess match; it's not even a dialogue except in the limited sense that an exchange occurs between two individuals. A fight is a fight, although in the more interesting ones a man's skill, courage, and grace can make us briefly forget the end to which they are being put.

Who Speaks
for the Lazy?

For a white American male in good health and in possession of an advanced degree from an Ivy League school, I have, over the past twenty-five years, made a ridiculously small amount of money. And when I say small, I mean *small*. I don't want to get into numbers; let's just say that when I was called to the IRS office about twenty years ago to structure a payment schedule for back taxes, the agent, after toting up earnings and expenses, leaned over and gave my arm a sympathetic pat. Being a writer only partially explains this woeful fiscal history. The real question is not so much how I've managed to survive but why I have accepted living in humble circumstances when my tastes are anything but. It's a question that friends, for whom my way of life has often been a subject of rueful and hilarious conversation, have speculated on. Here are some of the answers they've come up with: came of age in the sixties; never came of age; has an aversion to authority; has a structural anomaly of the brain; lost his mother when he was ten; was an only child; was an only child of parents who survived the war in Europe; read too many books at too early an age; found a really cheap, rent-stabilized apartment; is generally a moody, shiftless, self-absorbed individual.

Not making a lot of money says something about a man in a society where financial success is equated with acumen, resourcefulness, and social standing. Aside from those who enter professions in which money is not the main consideration – teaching, say, or diplomacy, or documentary filmmaking – the non-moneyed are thought to lack the confidence or wherewithal to make the big bucks. There is an assumption that a feeling of ineligibility keeps us from realizing the earning potential both in ourselves and in the marketplace. It is, of course, just this entrepreneurial inner child that self-help books mean to awaken. True or not, success American-style is seen to be a matter of gumption, of get-up-and-go: economic hardship isn't about race or class, it's about character. Want money? Follow the appropriate twelve-step program, demonstrate the requisite stick-to-itiveness, and – badda badda bing – you're rolling in it.

Although it would be nice to say that the absence of a portfolio in my case suggested a well-developed ego, an indifference to the world's approval, I'm afraid that emotional immaturity as well as financial shortsightedness are nearer the mark. When I was in my twenties, it didn't matter that other men my age earned eighty grand a year while I survived on eight. I was healthy, strong, O.K.-looking, with a good head of hair (never discount male vanity as consolation for practically anything). There'd be time, I thought, to remedy matters. And let's be clear: I did not disdain the dollar. I was no ascetic, and my spiritual itch was more than satisfied by reading Hermann Hesse. In truth, I was materialistic to the core: I loved money; I loved the idea of money; I even liked novels about the rich and movies about how the poor became rich. I liked everything about money except the prospect of buckling down and making it.

My father used to say that I became a writer so that I wouldn't have to work. Most writers will snort at this; what is writing *but* work? He had a point, though. The thought of being bound and defined by work that didn't interest me sent shivers down my spine. The solution was a string of part-time jobs that I could blow off whenever I wanted to — until I made it as a writer. Between 1971 and 1981, I drove a cab, hefted sacks of grain in an animal-feed warehouse, served time as a night watchman in a rundown hotel, lifted boxes on and off a conveyer belt, tutored philosophy, worked construction, loaded and unloaded trucks for UPS, and hauled freight along the Louisville-Cincinnati-Lexington triangle. None of these jobs paid more than four dollars an hour, and until 1992 I had no bank account: no checking, no savings. Also no car, no credit cards, no cashmere socks.

Sometimes I moved from one city to another simply because I had the chance to house-sit or because a friend offered to put me up. I don't defend, and I most certainly don't recommend, this way of life. It may, in fact, no longer be feasible, given today's success-oriented ethos and the way prices have risen. In the mid-seventies, a quart of milk cost thirty cents in Boston; a carton of cigarettes, two dollars in South Carolina; filet mignon, four dollars a pound in Kentucky. One of the best Chambertins I ever drank set me back seventeen dollars in New Jersey.

Looking back, my peripatetic, hand-to-mouth existence puzzles more than it embarrasses me. Why did I settle for so little when I wanted so much more? And yet at the time it seemed like the life I should lead. Not because I wanted to be a writer (it wasn't as if the words to *"Vissi d'arte"* filled my head) but because I saw myself – and this is where it does get a little embarrassing – in the light of books I had read as a teenager. I was great for poets and poetry and for whatever seemed fantastic, romantic, and tragic in books. I didn't exactly identify with Marlowe, Coleridge, Byron, Keats, Poe, Baudelaire, Rimbaud, and Pushkin, but their examples did make me feel that hewing to the straight and narrow would somehow be disloyal to their own fervid imaginings.

One of the dangers of reading the right books at the wrong age is the tendency to confuse the creator with the creation. Since Des Esseintes, Pechorin, Stavrogin, Julian Sorel, Maldoror, and the Corsair could have been given shape only by men very much like themselves, I decided around the age of fourteen to become a blasé voluptuary, a weary adventurer who traveled the world over, conquering women and boredom. This foolishness didn't last long, but for a time words and expressions like "anomie," "ennui," "spleen," "melancholy," and "alienated consciousness" made it difficult for me to think practically about the future.

But to say that I avoided long-term employment merely out of some misguided application of literature to life (where Emma Bovary sought liaisons, I sought leisure) would be preposterous. I never wanted to work. Even as a kid, I thought working for money, whether I needed it or not, was a bad trade-off. In 1960, planted in front of an old RCA console, I warmed to the ersatz beatnik Maynard G. Krebs on *The Many Loves of Dobie Gillis,* who on hearing the word "work" would involuntarily yelp "Work!" as if an angry bee had suddenly dived into view. I didn't want to be Maynard G. Krebs, but then I didn't want to be much of anything. That annoying question kids have to contend with – "What do you want to be when you grow up?" – left me stupefied.

Not that I didn't have ambition. I had plans: I was going to write big, fat novels and make potloads of money. But what good is ambition without energy? It's nothing more than daydreaming. Novels demand drive and Trollope-like commitment. Naturally, I wasn't up to it, although I did manage to become a literary journalist and a regular contributor to various publications. Yet even as a recognized member of a guild, I was a spectacular non-go-getter. You would not have seen my shining face at conferences, panel discussions, readings, parties, or wherever else editors, agents, and publishers showed up. Networking and self-promotion, the hallmarks of literary aspirants, demand hustle, and hustling, among other things, means moving briskly. I stayed home. I wrote about books, literary trends, academic criticism. And though I occasionally took on an assignment to write about boxing or business (experience obviously not required), my earnings pretty much stayed on an even keel. I wrote book reviews for the *money*.

Some men are born lazy, some acquire laziness, some have laziness thrust upon them. But, however gained, laziness remains ill gotten. Because we make a virtue of what is necessary, the precept of work is like a commandment *sans* stone tablet. It's man's nature to work; without work, people tend to wilt. On the other hand, some people droop by design. Look at small children: not all are animated tykes scampering about the playground; there are always one or two likely to sit by themselves, ruminating on the fact that they have ten fingers and toes instead of nine or eleven. They are the suspect ones, the nascent lazy, and, left to their own devices, will probably not metamorphose into the movers and shakers of their generation.

Although laziness in its simplest terms is the disinclination to work, the condition is not reducible to a simple formula. For most of recorded history, laziness was thought to arise from the natural confluence of mind and body. The lazy suffered from melancholia, or an excess of black bile (carried by the blood to the brain), which in extreme cases kept them from finding solace in spiritual devotions. Those in whom the spirit failed to move or to be moved were afflicted with acedia – a condition that the early Church fathers felt deserved a measure of compassion, along with the usual tsk-tsking. But as the world grew older, and time got tangled up with the idea of "progress," work and busyness, rather than piety, took on antonymic meaning where laziness was concerned. By the late Middle Ages, acedia had come to include the notion of worldly sloth. And who was responsible for sloth? You were. Sloth didn't just slide into the world along with your squalling body; you had to seek it out and embrace it. There was a reason that sloth eventually replaced melancholy as one of the seven deadly sins.

As a secular sin, laziness reached its apogee during the Industrial Revolution, when any sign of malingering was seen as a threat to the capitalist order. If you didn't work, you didn't produce, and if you didn't produce you were a parasite; you were, my friend, subversive. Don't get me wrong: I'm not defending the lazy. All I'm saying is that the subject makes people take extreme views. When Boswell suggested that "we grow weary when idle," the otherwise sensible Dr. Johnson remonstrated, "That is, sir, because others being busy, we want company; but if we were idle, there would be no growing weary; we should all entertain one another." Is he kidding? The man obviously never hung out with the deadbeat crowd I used to know, for whom prying the cap off a Schlitz was a good day's work. Most people disdain the lazy not only because they serve no useful purpose but because their own metabolisms and circadian rhythms seem to recognize those whose systems are out of sync. The lazy are different from you and me. I mean, of course, just you.

Medically, however, I'm fine. Two blood tests, years apart, revealed no bacterial parasites or high concentrations of viral antibodies, or any other noxious agents that could account for my usual indolence. No toxins in the air, no food groups, no glowing chunks of kryptonite rob me of my powers. Nor, when I look around, can I lay the blame on the sixties, or on my being an only child, or on my retreating into books at a tender age, or, for that matter, on family history. Although the early death of a parent so constricts the heart that it can never regain its original shape, plenty of children suffer loss and sadness and go on to lead busy, productive lives.

Sometimes the only good explanation for the arc life takes is that a person has only so much spring in his step, that one is born to travel only so far. And, while most of us want to get to the top, not all of us are willing to make the climb. My father wasn't entirely mistaken in claiming that I turned to writing in order to avoid work. Let's face it, some boys and girls become writers because the only workplace they're willing to visit is the one inside their heads. And even then it's a tough commute, since the same urge that leads them to write may also keep them from doing their work. That general discontent with the world that is at the bottom of all writing tends to pull writers down, deplete them of initiative, and make them wonder if it's worth doing at all. This applies as well to writers who churn out prose at a ferocious clip as it does to those who, like Bartleby, prefer not to. The trick is to turn that urge to one's advantage. "I write of melancholy, by being busy to avoid melancholy," wrote the industrious Robert Burton.

Likewise, writers who know themselves to be lazy con-
scientiously and routinely meet their inertia head-on. Profound laziness is not so much about doing nothing as it is
about the strain of doing practically *anything*. Lazy people
can accomplish things, thank you very much. We have our
paroxysms of activity, the occasional eruptions of busyness
and bursts of productivity. Walter Benjamin, for instance,
acknowledged that he had entered "the world under the sign
of Saturn – the star of the slowest revolution, the planet of
detours and delays," yet the man's formidable essays didn't,
as they say, write themselves. Our first essayist, Montaigne,
also professed to have a wide streak of laziness, and Cyril
Connolly, whose journal *Horizon* helped keep English letters afloat during World War II, gloated, "Others merely
live; I vegetate."

But vegetation among writers and thinkers takes peculiar forms. Someone who sits and conjures up names and
explanations for characters or subatomic particles cannot
be said to be doing nothing. A world of difference exists
between a valetudinarian fused to his bed and Max Beerbohm, who never voluntarily went out for a walk, because
"it stops the brain." Still, the standard, hackneyed concep-
tion of laziness prevails. "Doomed as I was to a life of perpetual idleness, I did absolutely nothing," says the landscape
painter in Chekhov's story "The House with the Attic."
"I spent hours looking out of the window at the sky, the
birds, the avenues, read everything that was brought to me
from the post, and slept. Sometimes I left the house and
went for walks till late at night." Yes, yes, we've heard all
this before. Don't be fooled: there's no uniformity about the
lazy. Energetic people may be all alike, but the lazy cruise
along at their own varying rates of speed. Some bite the
bullet and go off to jobs; some stay home while their more
energetic spouses tackle the workaday world; some really

do watch the grass grow, or, its millennial equivalent, daytime television.

180   There is something preemptive about laziness, something that smacks of a decision to refuse all offers even before they're put on the table. The lazy don't come to the table. And I think there is a philosophical component to this reluctance. At bottom, laziness is negation, turning one's back on what others neutrally, cheerfully, or resignedly go to meet. The truly lazy – the ones who cannot bring themselves to greet and meet, to scheme and struggle, to interact on a daily basis with others – are, in effect, refusing to affix their signatures to the social contract. Given that success hinges on understanding, using, and occasionally subverting the social contract, the lazy don't stand a chance.

The secret to failure is far more elusive than the secret to success. Lagging behind when one could have advanced isn't just about laziness; it's about all the things that psychoanalysis takes a rather serious view of – the absence of love, coping with anger, rationalizing failure, the reluctance to supersede or replace one's father. Heavy stuff, and perhaps true, but the acknowledgment of which never put a dime in my pocket.

Laziness just is. It's like being freckled or color blind. Indeed, when the world was younger, intelligent people believed they had no choice in the matter of who was naughty or nice, passive or active. Hippocrates's theory of "temperament," which anchored Western medicine for two millennia, put some muscle behind varieties of human behavior. Well, not muscle exactly – more like four potentially pathogenic substances, or cardinal humors, whose relative proportion in the blood determined personality and moods. The Church fathers, as it turns out, were on the right track; only the messenger and manner of delivery were wrong. It's not black bile or phlegm that causes Oblomov-like symptoms but a certain kind of electrochemical activity in the left frontal lobe of the brain, or whatever. The point is, everyone enters the world predisposed physiologically to think and feel in certain ways.

Happenstance also has its place; I don't deny that. But do any two people react identically to the same stimuli? The event that jump-starts one person's psyche does not necessarily have the same effect on another's. It's one thing to concede that certain tendencies can be reinforced or weakened by experience; it is quite another to think that some event during my formative years, which might have occurred but didn't, would have had me sharing a bucket of Kentucky Fried Chicken with Bill Gates, or loping down a runway in Milan wearing a spiffy outfit by Valentino. In short, there's no contradiction in thinking that temperament defines you and thinking that you're still in charge of your life. Temperament is the gas, but you've got a foot on the pedal.

Because of some unpredictable sequence of recombinant DNA and early experiences, I always knew I'd write things. I also knew I was an incurable lazybones. This accounts, in my case, for the odd tension between writing and laziness, which Samuel Beckett describes to a T: "There is nothing to express, nothing with which to express, nothing from which to express, no power to express, no desire to express, together with the obligation to express." As a solid constituent of the couchant class, I can say that the obligation to express does not weigh heavily. Still, I have my moments – moments when I feel like addressing the fading shimmer of my own skin. I want answers. Or, more precisely, one big answer. In a sense, life is like an examination that has only one question – the one that asks why you're taking the exam in the first place. Having been instructed to "fill in the blank" (an aptly phrased command), you ponder, and then wonder if perhaps the truest answer is no answer at all. But in the end, because there is, after all, plenty of time to reflect and you do want to leave the room, you hunker down and fill in the blank. My own response is hardly profound or incisive: I'm taking the exam because I like writing sentences, and because – well, what else do I have to do?

As for the laziness that moves with me wherever I go, I have finally found a way to make it "work" for me. Lassitude, aloofness, low-grade depression, coupled with a healthy respect for money, have gradually steered me to the obvious vocation. Yes, dear reader, I have become a screenwriter.

ACKNOWLEDGMENTS

By some strange coincidence, the more one improves as a writer, the better one's editors turn out to be. Such eerie design in the universe has allowed me to work with Anne Fadiman and Jean Stipicevic at the *American Scholar*; John J. Sullivan and Jennifer Szalai at *Harper's*; and Henry Finder, Leo Carey, and Mary Hawthorne at the *New Yorker*. For careful readings and fearless advice, I thank Evelyn Toynton and Joy Adzegian.

CREDITS

"The Amazing Ordinary Writing Machine" appeared as "Against Type." *Harper's*. December 2002.

"The Pages of Sin." *Harper's*. January 2005.

"An African American in Regency England" appeared in abridged form as "Requiem for a Heavyweight." *The New Yorker*. July 20, 1998.

"Hello, Beautiful! *Harper's*. September 2005.

"My Holocaust Problem." *The American Scholar*. Autumn. 2005.

"The Inexhaustible Paul Valéry" appeared as "Poet in the Machine." *Harper's*. February 2004.

"Club Work." Introduction to *A Company of Readers: The Uncollected Writings of W. H. Auden, Jacques Barzun, and Lionel Trilling from The Readers' Subscription and Mid-Century Book Clubs*. The Free Press. August 2001.

"No Failure Like Success: The Life of Raymond Chandler." *The American Scholar*. Summer 1996.

"Here's Looking At You" is a composite of pieces culled from *The American Scholar* (Autumn 2004), *The New York Times Book Review* (July 12, 1987), and *Art & Antiques* (February 1994).

"Boxers and Writers" appeared as "Ifs, Ands, Butts." *Harper's*. June 1987.

"Who Speaks for the Lazy?" *The New Yorker*. April 26 & May 3, 1999.